I0031235

Business Models in Emerging Technologies

Business Models in Emerging Technologies

Data Science, AI, and Blockchain

Stylianos Kampakis

Theodosis Mourouzis

Gerard Cardoso

Marialena Zinopoulou

BEP

BUSINESS EXPERT PRESS

Leader in applied, concise business books

Business Models in Emerging Technologies:
Data Science, AI, and Blockchain

Copyright © Business Expert Press, LLC, 2023.

Cover design by Charlene Kronstedt

Interior design by Exeter Premedia Services Private Ltd., Chennai, India

All rights reserved. No part of this publication may be reproduced, stored in a retrieval system, or transmitted in any form or by any means—electronic, mechanical, photocopy, recording, or any other except for brief quotations, not to exceed 400 words, without the prior permission of the publisher.

First published in 2022 by
Business Expert Press, LLC
222 East 46th Street, New York, NY 10017
www.businessexpertpress.com

ISBN-13: 978-1-63742-313-4 (paperback)
ISBN-13: 978-1-63742-314-1 (e-book)

Business Expert Press Big Data, Business Analytics, and Smart Technology Collection

First edition: 2022

10 9 8 7 6 5 4 3 2 1

Business Models in Emerging Technologies

Data Science, AI, and Blockchain

Stylianos Kampakis

Theodosis Mourouzis

Gerard Cardoso

Marialena Zinopoulou

BEP

BUSINESS EXPERT PRESS

Leader in applied, concise business books

Business Models in Emerging Technologies:
Data Science, AI, and Blockchain

Copyright © Business Expert Press, LLC, 2023.

Cover design by Charlene Kronstedt

Interior design by Exeter Premedia Services Private Ltd., Chennai, India

All rights reserved. No part of this publication may be reproduced, stored in a retrieval system, or transmitted in any form or by any means—electronic, mechanical, photocopy, recording, or any other except for brief quotations, not to exceed 400 words, without the prior permission of the publisher.

First published in 2022 by
Business Expert Press, LLC
222 East 46th Street, New York, NY 10017
www.businessexpertpress.com

ISBN-13: 978-1-63742-313-4 (paperback)
ISBN-13: 978-1-63742-314-1 (e-book)

Business Expert Press Big Data, Business Analytics, and Smart Technology Collection

First edition: 2022

10 9 8 7 6 5 4 3 2 1

Description

The world of technology progresses so quickly that we often don't realize how far we've come. Over the last 20 years, technologies such as data science, artificial intelligence, the Internet of Things, and blockchain have transformed the world of business, industry, and society.

These emerging technologies offer a wide range of opportunities. However, they also create new challenges businesses must face, such as developing new business models, discovering the best adoption strategies, designing the best digital transformation strategies, and more.

This book is a practical guide to two of the most important emerging technologies: data science/AI and blockchain. With broad applicability across all sectors, decision makers would greatly benefit from understanding these fields. And that is why we cover a wide range of topics in an easy-to-access manner that everyone can understand.

This book contains it all, from easy-to-understand descriptions of the technologies themselves to more in-depth explanations on how they can be used. Other topics this book covers include data strategy, business models to start new AI-based businesses, types of blockchain, data science processes, and much more.

After reading this book, you'll have a much better understanding of how you can use data science/AI and blockchain in your business to create transformation, improvements, and positive change.

Keywords

artificial intelligence; AI; blockchain; machine learning; data science; data strategy; business model; emerging tech

Contents

List of Figures

List of Figures

List of Tables

Foreword

We are currently drowning in data! The data management pyramid, also known as the DIKW pyramid, examines the hierarchical relationship between data, information, knowledge, and wisdom as shown in Figure F.1. We note that there is a distinct hierarchy in the level of analysis of data. If we translate this for the business of tomorrow, we could have the pyramid showing impact at the base, followed by intelligence that leads to insights and finally innovation (Figure F.2). The first level would include any data that has an **Impact** on the business. The analysis of that data in depth would yield **Intelligence** that can be collated into valuable **Insights** and used to inform the next level of business **Innovation.**

Currently, we have analytics tools available that can help analyze data to obtain basic information. But unfortunately, that is not always enough. Discovering that the target audience is 21 to 24-year-olds living in the United Kingdom and using at least two social media platforms daily is an example of the basic information we can pull from data. However, using this kind of information as the basis for business decisions can be like trying to analyze a book's storyline and characters based on two or three chapters.

Reaching the next level of data analysis is not easy. Getting valuable insights from data is a Herculean task. We often lack the expertise to do

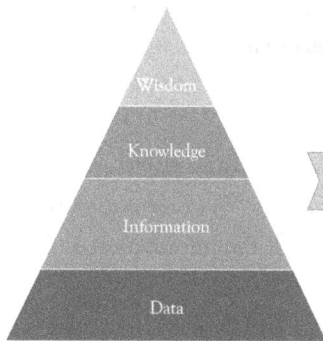

Figure F.1 The DIKW pyramid   *Figure F.2 Business analytics pyramid*

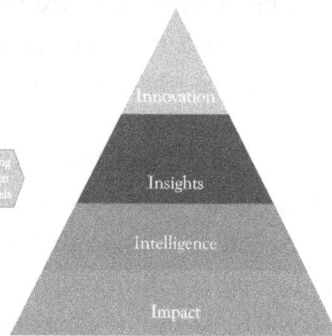

so, and that is because insights are not reported in a tool or presented in a report somewhere. To convert information into actionable insights, one needs to know how to collect data from multiple sources and then connect the dots that translate into meaningful knowledge. And we need true insights to be able to utilize data. The growth of the Internet of Things (IoT) and 5G technology will see more connected devices than ever before and the flow of real-time data as a result. As consumers begin to rely on wearables while becoming more immersed in digital experiences, we will have to find new ways to measure the impact that those experiences leave. New metrics will emerge as vital in understanding behavior patterns, and we will have to find more advanced ways for understanding what the data is saying.

The consensus in the business world today is that we need to be better at analyzing our data. The issue at hand is how? Data scientists today work with data to create these insights, and businesses benefit from clear and actionable results from data analysis. However, this will not be possible when we consider the volume and sources of the data we will deal with. To take the business to that next level of data analysis, we can turn to emerging technologies, specifically artificial intelligence (AI).

AI can help solve the problem of analyzing data in motion—this is data coming in real time—as it can process information and analyze thousands of pieces of information drawn from multiple levels and from varied sources, which can yield "live" results within seconds. Therefore, implementing AI-powered insights can change the way we do marketing and how we make strategic decisions.

We do, however, also need to make sure the results are explainable. A business needs to understand how the intelligence was used to give the resulting insights. We need a clear concept of why we are getting these results.

Explainable AI for business will be an important consideration in the implementation process of new business models. This means understanding the connections and associations that link the information and why the AI system saw them as significant.

It will be essential to ensure there are no broken links in the data and information that is used or misalignment in the objectives that the AI applies. It will also be valuable from an ethical point of view to ensure that there is accountability and to avoid bias in the decision-making process when business insights are based on AI analysis.

As we find ourselves at the dawn of the Fourth Industrial Revolution, we know that the line between the physical, digital, and virtual worlds will become blurred as they are linked together through IoT sensors and simulators. As a result, we will become a more cyber society.

This industrial revolution is going to be more powerful than the previous ones. We are no longer dealing with just one new technology but with multiple powerful emerging technologies that are all interlinked and can work together. These technologies are just as powerful and impactful as electricity was 150 years ago or the Internet was 40 years ago. And just like when electricity and the Internet were introduced, the world will never be the same again.

This time, however, we have an entirely new phenomenon taking place. We don't have just one, but multiple emerging technologies all introduced at once. AI, blockchain, augmented and virtual reality, and the IoT will change every aspect of life as we know it. It is predicted that it will be many times more impactful than any previous industrial revolution.

A change like that will see the introduction of new ways of doing things. It will mean new business models, communication channels, and immersive social environments. Businesses need to stay informed with the changing landscape and plan ahead. A strong understanding of the impact that these technologies will have on their customers and their business will ensure that they start to find ways to implement strategies in time.

A business that doesn't understand customer journey analytics (2–5 years from plateau of productivity) and social analytics (less than two years from plateau of productivity), based on the Gartner Hype Cycle for Digital Marketing in 2021 (Gartner 2021), is likely to be left behind when this analysis is required to reach and understand the target audience. Real-time marketing is 5 to 10 years away, according to the same hype cycle (Gartner 2021), which indicates that businesses should know how to analyze data in real time to do real-time marketing effectively by the end of this decade. For a company to be ready to collect, secure, and analyze data on impact, we need to fully understand these technologies and their capabilities.

Data scientists have been working on understanding how businesses can utilize emerging technologies and find solutions to suggest applications and new business models that will help with the implementation and analysis. However, many companies are still in the dark, and alarm bells are ringing that time is running out. The need to evolve quickly to stay relevant in the world of tomorrow should be top on the strategic agenda.

We can visualize emerging technologies as working as the human body does. AI is the brain where information is processed and analyzed to give us knowledge and insights that lead to wisdom. Virtual reality and augmented/mixed reality are the senses—a way to see and appreciate new content and environments that immerse us into new experiences. Blockchain is our immune system—the chain of protection that secures the system. The IoT is the nervous system, where multiple sensors collect information and send it to the brain for processing. Finally, 5G is the fuel that keeps it all running—like glucose in the body. And just like our body works as one connected system, with each part relying on the other, so too do these technologies rely on each other for information, analysis, security, and fuel.

Emerging technologies will change how we communicate, work, educate, live, socialize, and do business. We can prepare by understanding the implications and working toward new business models that will inspire innovation.

—Dr. M Zinopoulou

there is accountability and to avoid bias in the decision-making process when business insights are based on AI analysis.

As we find ourselves at the dawn of the Fourth Industrial Revolution, we know that the line between the physical, digital, and virtual worlds will become blurred as they are linked together through IoT sensors and simulators. As a result, we will become a more cyber society.

This industrial revolution is going to be more powerful than the previous ones. We are no longer dealing with just one new technology but with multiple powerful emerging technologies that are all interlinked and can work together. These technologies are just as powerful and impactful as electricity was 150 years ago or the Internet was 40 years ago. And just like when electricity and the Internet were introduced, the world will never be the same again.

This time, however, we have an entirely new phenomenon taking place. We don't have just one, but multiple emerging technologies all introduced at once. AI, blockchain, augmented and virtual reality, and the IoT will change every aspect of life as we know it. It is predicted that it will be many times more impactful than any previous industrial revolution.

A change like that will see the introduction of new ways of doing things. It will mean new business models, communication channels, and immersive social environments. Businesses need to stay informed with the changing landscape and plan ahead. A strong understanding of the impact that these technologies will have on their customers and their business will ensure that they start to find ways to implement strategies in time.

A business that doesn't understand customer journey analytics (2–5 years from plateau of productivity) and social analytics (less than two years from plateau of productivity), based on the Gartner Hype Cycle for Digital Marketing in 2021 (Gartner 2021), is likely to be left behind when this analysis is required to reach and understand the target audience. Real-time marketing is 5 to 10 years away, according to the same hype cycle (Gartner 2021), which indicates that businesses should know how to analyze data in real time to do real-time marketing effectively by the end of this decade. For a company to be ready to collect, secure, and analyze data on impact, we need to fully understand these technologies and their capabilities.

Data scientists have been working on understanding how businesses can utilize emerging technologies and find solutions to suggest applications and new business models that will help with the implementation and analysis. However, many companies are still in the dark, and alarm bells are ringing that time is running out. The need to evolve quickly to stay relevant in the world of tomorrow should be top on the strategic agenda.

We can visualize emerging technologies as working as the human body does. AI is the brain where information is processed and analyzed to give us knowledge and insights that lead to wisdom. Virtual reality and augmented/mixed reality are the senses—a way to see and appreciate new content and environments that immerse us into new experiences. Blockchain is our immune system—the chain of protection that secures the system. The IoT is the nervous system, where multiple sensors collect information and send it to the brain for processing. Finally, 5G is the fuel that keeps it all running—like glucose in the body. And just like our body works as one connected system, with each part relying on the other, so too do these technologies rely on each other for information, analysis, security, and fuel.

Emerging technologies will change how we communicate, work, educate, live, socialize, and do business. We can prepare by understanding the implications and working toward new business models that will inspire innovation.

—Dr. M Zinopoulou

CHAPTER 1

What Are Emerging Technologies?

We are in the midst of what many are calling the "Fourth Industrial Revolution." With so many emerging technologies that are changing our society, it's an accurate description. And, like the three previous industrial revolutions, our world will evolve to a completely new level.

But what are emerging technologies?

Emerging technologies represent any technology with massive potential that hasn't been fully realized. It can be old or new tech. The key is that it can completely change society, either through its development or application.

Gene therapy is an example of an older technology that can still be classed as emerging tech. Developed in the early 1990s, gene therapy still has a lot of potential that hasn't been explored.

More recent innovations that are classed as emerging technologies include artificial intelligence (AI)/data science, blockchain, Internet of Things (IoT), 3D printing, 5G, quantum computing, and robotics (Figure 1.1). These are all technologies that are still in their infancy. Yet, they have already significantly changed the world we live in.

As these technologies evolve, the degree of change will amplify until we reach a point where society will be completely different from even a few years ago. A quick look at history proves that this is exactly what will happen.

The History of Technological Disruption

Humanity's history is peppered with technological disruption. Throughout our existence, technology has played a significant role in our society.

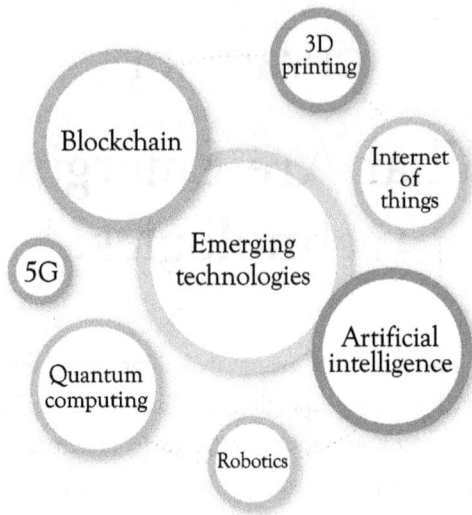

Figure 1.1 Emerging technologies

From humanity's invention of the wheel and the development of agriculture to the harnessing of electricity and the invention of computers, many of our significant leaps of societal progress can be attributed to technological progress.

Take the First Industrial Revolution. Starting around 1760, it introduced mechanical production, thanks to the invention of the steam engine. Suddenly, people didn't have to do everything by hand. Steam-powered machines could do a lot of the hard work—they could also do it faster and often better.

People could also travel faster and more easily, thanks to steamships and trains, basically making the world a smaller place. It also saw the rise of the middle class.

Then came the Second Industrial Revolution, where things such as petrol engines, chemical fertilizers, and airplanes once again changed the world. This was also the age of mass production, making it easier for people to get what they needed.

And since people always follow employment, there was a significant migration of the population from rural to urban centers.

How people lived also changed. Things such as electric lighting, the radio, and the telephone transformed society.

The Third Industrial Revolution was dubbed the Digital Revolution and started in the 1950s. It saw the rise of semiconductors, personal computing, and the Internet.

The shift from analog to digital changed the world in ways no one could have expected. Every industry was affected, including global communications, energy, and manufacturing.

Think of mobile phones. They completely changed society. Before mobile phones, if something happened and you weren't in reach of a telephone (like getting a flat tire in the middle of nowhere), one had to hope someone would come along who could help.

Now? All one has to do is whip their phone out and call for assistance. Of course, that's if the car itself hasn't already alerted the service provider of the problem. Then again, that is IoT, so we're getting a bit ahead of ourselves.

Nevertheless, the past two decades alone have seen society change massively to what it once was. And all that is due to technological progress, which leads us into the Fourth Industrial Revolution.

The Fourth Industrial Revolution: Sci-Fi Coming to Reality

The Fourth Industrial Revolution is likely to be the biggest one yet. Previous revolutions centered around a few major inventions that drove others, in a domino effect, like the steam engine drove the First Industrial Revolution.

Now, we have a somewhat different situation. We have multiple emerging technologies that will not only each drive advancements but will also work together to create even more progress and change.

One thing that won't change, though, is the danger of failing to adapt. Businesses that aren't prepared to change and avoid adopting new tech will disappear.

Historically, those that didn't adopt steam engines and stuck to their ways couldn't compete. The same happened to companies that didn't take advantage of the developments of the Second and Third Industrial Revolutions.

Likewise, businesses that do not evolve and get left behind in the race for tech adoption will experience the same fate, especially since we live in a consumer-driven world where the consumer is becoming increasingly tech-savvy, and expectations have skyrocketed.

Let's take a quick look at some of the emerging technologies driving the Fourth Industrial Revolution.

AI/Data Science

The business world has evolved, moving past making decisions based on people's digestive systems. Big Data is now primarily driving decision making.

However, Big Data is getting bigger every day, which makes analysis more challenging. And that is where AI comes in.

Without AI systems to analyze all that data, companies would be stuck with a slew of information that, in essence, would be useless. And without insights derived from the raw data, decisions would continue to be as gut-based as ever.

AI isn't just being used to provide better insights, either, as machine learning (ML) solutions are increasingly being used in manufacturing and industrial settings to make decisions. From adjusting the working parameters of a machine on a production line to scheduling maintenance for a piece of equipment in an industrial facility to running simulations on a digital twin to identify failure points, ML algorithms are becoming an increasingly important part of Industry 4.0.

One of the biggest applications of AI and ML in an Industry 4.0 context is in the area of market demand management. Anticipating future market demand typically involves analyzing historical data. With AI and ML tools, however, manufacturers will be able to go much further.

A ML algorithm can look at things such as weather patterns, major events, socioeconomic issues, and consumer behavior to make assessments on market demand for products before they hit the production line.

The ML algorithm can then use this analysis to optimize everything from staffing to inventory to raw material purchasing to ensure optimal performance. As these ML tools become more widespread, they will have a game-changing impact on the manufacturing industry.

Blockchain

Blockchain has already started to change retail, government, banking, and many more sectors. By decentralizing systems, blockchain eliminates many inefficiencies and, more importantly, creates never-before-seen transparency.

Unsurprisingly, blockchain is driving change simply by existing. For example, even if traditional financial organizations haven't jumped on the blockchain bandwagon, they've had to improve their services to remain competitive.

In terms of Industry 4.0, blockchain technologies have transformative potential in a range of areas. One example is supply chain management, where blockchain technologies can improve transparency, reduce risks, and cut processes that traditionally take days or weeks down to minutes or hours.

By using blockchain technologies, products can be monitored in real time as they move through the supply chain, with no risk of someone trying to alter, for example, a completion or delivery date. Delays in communication can also be minimized as everyone in the supply chain can have access to the same information at the same time, reducing the need for ineffective and inefficient communication methods such as e-mail.

Financial transactions in the supply chain can also be streamlined with the additional benefit of maximum transparency. Again, this can help to eliminate delays caused by communication inefficiencies and human error.

Other applications for the blockchain in the factory of the future include:

- Quality control—where each component, manufacturing process, and assembly process is stored in the blockchain along with multiple other data points, from temperatures to humidity levels to dates and more.
- Traceability—traceability is a key process in many industries, and it is becoming more important, even when regulations don't require it. Blockchain offers a decentralized and highly efficient method of ensuring product traceability throughout the full product life cycle.

- Compliance—compliance is a major consideration in industries such as pharmaceuticals and food production, and companies are always looking for ways to streamline their compliance processes. New blockchain technologies have the potential to achieve these efficiency savings.
- Fraud prevention—product fraud is a major issue for a range of industries, from clothing manufacturers to pharmaceuticals. The un-editable nature of blockchain technologies makes them ideally suited for the creation of new fraud prevention tools to help protect the manufacturing sector.

IoT

The IoT is turning sci-fi into reality. "Smart" equipment that transfers data without the need for human input is revolutionizing the way we do everything.

From heart monitor implants keeping people healthy to refrigerators that can order groceries, IoT is changing how we live and do business.

Another example of how IoT technologies are transforming business in the Industry 4.0 era is R&D and new product development. In the past, product development teams would be forced to use incomplete and often inaccurate data, as well as subjective opinions, to determine the focus for future development. With the IoT, product developers can get real-time information on exactly how people are using products, as well as on how well those products are performing. This will lead to a much more user-first approach to product development across all industries.

There is also the Industrial Internet of Things (IIoT). It is an extension of the IoT as it focuses on the technologies that apply to industrial and manufacturing environments. As with the IoT, the IIoT is about connecting a range of different devices, equipment, and machines in an industrial setting.

However, where the IIoT is making the biggest impact is in narrowing the gap between IT (information technology) and OT (operational technology).

Traditionally in the manufacturing sector, IT and OT were completely separate, with little connectivity or integration. So, for example,

Customer Relationship Management (CRM), accounting, and sales apps that are part of IT would have no integration with the equipment, systems, and platforms that produce the products on the factory floor.

IIoT technologies are playing an important role in facilitating the integration of IT and IIoT, improving productivity, efficiency, and oversight in manufacturing organizations.

3D Printing

3D printing has already disrupted multiple industries. In health care, medical professionals are printing prosthetics and replicas of bones, organs, and blood vessels, all tailored to a specific patient.

It can also help reduce waste, build homes for everyone, provide clothing, feed the homeless, and more.

Essentially, this is a technology that, when combined with all the other emerging tech, can eventually lead us to making whatever we need with the push of a button, from vehicles to food.

Even simple applications are being transformed by 3D printing, such as producing a prototype of product currently being developed. 3D-printed prototypes can be produced in a fraction of the time and at a fraction of the cost with less costly equipment. This is just one other example of how 3D printing really is a gamechanger.

5G Technology

5G is already taking the world by storm as it offers faster speeds, more capacity, and reduced latency for mobile networks. In other words, more data can be transferred at much higher speeds, which will drive significant change in our society.

For example, it could help improve public safety in emergencies. The ability to handle higher volumes of high-quality video means that authorities can more effectively analyze emergencies, thereby leading to more effective responses.

5G technology is also a key driver of the IoT, plus it enables highly innovative edge computing solutions. Those edge computing solutions don't just mean data can be collected from almost anywhere.

5G technology also means that data can also be processed at the edge, improving performance.

There are multiple reasons why 5G is important to Industry 4.0. First, 5G enables faster communication between systems, platforms, and equipment. This reduces latency to a point that is close to wired connections, so helps to optimize production processes where physical connections are impractical.

5G technologies also make it possible to transmit critical communications reliably and in real time. This was not possible previously when the only option was 4G technologies. Not only does the reliability, speed, and low latency of 5G have productivity implications but also safety benefits.

Quantum Computing

Quantum computers will be able to solve many computationally impossible problems, which will revolutionize many industries.

For example, quantum computing can help scientists discover and develop new drugs much faster. At the same time, in finances, these systems can provide better analytics and help improve trading, data speed, and transactions.

While this technology is in its infancy, quantum computing has usage applications across a wide range of areas. Enhancing risk management is one example, as well as enabling manufacturers to achieve faster and more customer-centric production. Business strategies such as mass customization are set to become the norm as quantum computing develops further.

Quantum computing will also see the introduction of sensors that are smaller and more sensitive. This will not only have benefits for the products that manufacturing companies produce but it will also help to improve manufacturing processes, given the importance of sensors in developing smart factories.

Metrology is another area of manufacturing that quantum computing is predicted to have a significant impact. For many manufacturers, metrology is an essential driver for quality assurance and, by extension, optimizing manufacturing processes. Metrology technologies and solutions that utilize quantum computing will take the field to another level, providing manufacturing organizations with new data and insights, as well as achieving even greater levels of measurement accuracy and process repeatability.

Robotics

Progress in robotics is accelerating, and we've already seen automation implemented in the manufacturing industry, leading to increased efficiencies. But robotics continues to evolve and, as AI and ML progress, it won't be long before robots can take over many more of the jobs that humans have to do now.

As robots become more prevalent, productivity will rise, and the economy will grow. However, we will also see a shift in society as the types of jobs humans do will change.

One area of robotics that is rapidly advancing in the Industry 4.0 era is the development of robotic solutions that work alongside people. This type of equipment is often referred to as cobots. From autonomous vehicles to manufacturing and assembly lines, the efficiency gains that can be made with cobots and similar technologies is significant.

It isn't just efficiency and productivity gains, either, as cobots also have significant health and safety implications, helping to keep workers safe even in the harshest of conditions.

Then there is the concept of the lights-out factory, where robots are responsible for 100 percent of manufacturing and assembly processes, and are able to operate 24 hours a day, 7 days a week. They can do this without taking holidays, without making mistakes, and without getting tired or sick. We are still some distance away from this concept becoming a reality on anything like a widespread basis, and there are some who believe it won't be feasible. However, the lights out factory is the general direction of travel.

There are many reasons for this, and advances in robotic technologies are high up on that list. There are also other, more traditional considerations that are important too. Access to labor is one that can't be ignored. In many industries, upgrading production lines with robots isn't about replacing people. Instead, it is about changing a process because they are finding it increasingly difficult to recruit and train the right skills.

Summary

The Fourth Industrial Revolution is happening right now. This revolution is being driven by multiple technologies that are disrupting the world individually. However, when one combines these technologies, they will drive even greater levels of change.

Robotics is an excellent example. We started with robots that had to be programmed to perform the tiniest action. When we needed them to do something different, the code had to be changed. They certainly couldn't learn or think on their own. But AI and ML are changing that.

This book will focus on two of the biggest emerging technologies, namely AI/data science and blockchain. We'll look at what these emerging technologies are and how they're changing the world. The reason we focus on these is because they are the most popular ones, and they add the most value out of all other technologies. Indeed, while 5G is a great facilitator of telecommunications, and IoT generates massive amounts of data, they require methods borrowed from data science in order to generate value, and any applications of this kind can work synergistically with blockchain. Also, robotics can be seen as an application of AI, which is related to data science.

Therefore, these two technologies are what a decision maker really needs to know about right now.

We'll also be looking at why businesses need to adopt these technologies to remain competitive. After all, history proves that lagging in tech adoption will only lead to obscurity.

Key Takeaways

- The term "emerging technologies" refers to a group of technological advancements that have come to define industry 4.0.
- The key technologies of this revolution are: AI/data science and blockchain.

CHAPTER 2

An Introduction to Data Science/AI for the Nontechnical Person

In this chapter we will delve deeper into data science, and discuss what it is, and why it's useful. We will cover the brief history of data science and take a look at the core fields that compose it. The aim of this chapter is to give to the nontechnical reader a good brief overview of that area and understand where it can be applied and why.

Data science is made up of multiple disciplines. So, to get a good grasp of what data science is, we need to look at the core disciplines that make up this field of study. First, though, let's take a quick look at how it all started.

Brief History of Data Science

Though data science became more popular with the increase of data generation, it has been around for a while. Many look to John Tukey as one of the people who pushed the boundaries of statistics and gave birth to the concept of data analysis as a science (Leonhardt 2000).

Tukey wrote *The Future of Analysis* in 1962, while he was a professor at Princeton University and working at Bell Labs to develop statistical methods for computers (Tukey 1962).

In the article, he encouraged academic statisticians to get involved in the entire process of data analysis instead of just focusing on statistical theory. He pointed out how important it was to distinguish between exploratory and confirmatory data analysis, which was the first step to creating the field of data science.

While others certainly had a significant impact on data science as we know it today, Tukey was among the first to advocate for the importance of such a field. However, it took some time until the early 2000s for data science to really take off. The reason is that the turn of the millennium saw a few trends converging:

1. The rise of the Internet;
2. Cheaper storage and computing power;
3. The rise of cloud computing;
4. The rise in the volumes of data being generated.

The convergence of those four trends made data a valuable resource, with some calling data the new oil. This incentivized the re-emergence of the field of data science as a unifying force into what used to be disparate fields.

The Core Fields of Data Science

Taking a closer look at the history of data science means delving into its three core fields: AI, ML, and statistics. There are many other trends that have risen and fallen over the years: data mining, pattern recognition, cybernetics, and more. These terms often describe scientific approaches that tried to recreate intelligence inside a machine, or developed techniques to extract insights from data. However, the primary fields are AI, ML, and statistics, and we will delve into these in more depth over the next few chapters.

A Closer Look at AI

AI is exactly what it sounds like. People are trying to get machines to think like humans. In more technical terms, this means giving a machine the ability to reason logically, self-correct, and learn. Written out as it is, it might sound simple. It isn't. To even come vaguely close to achieving these goals, you need a lot of data and a lot of computing power.

Classic AI came into being in 1956 at Dartmouth College, when five men came together who would go on to become the founders and leaders of AI research. They were Allen Newell (CMU), Herbert Simon (CMU), John McCarthy (MIT), Marvin Minsky (MIT), and Arthur Samuel (IBM) (Russell, Norvig, and Davis 2010; McCorduck 2004).

It really started, though, with Marvin Minsky, who would become known as the father of AI. He wanted to create an intelligent

machine, which we would call AI and define it as the science of making machines perform tasks that would require intelligence if done by men (Whitby 1996).

To figure out how to achieve such a monumental goal, one must start by understanding the human brain, especially intuition, representing our capacity for logical reasoning.

Logical reasoning refers to the ability to draw logical conclusions based on various facts, such as:

"If all soldiers are in the army, and John is a soldier, then John is in the army."

This is a simple conclusion to draw for a human, of course. However, it's far more complicated for a machine to do it. To do so, humans constructed a set of rules with which they programmed the computer. Using this rule-based or symbolic approach, reasoning algorithms developed the ability to draw these logical conclusions. This gave birth to the rise of the "expert systems" market.

An early example of an expert system is MYCIN. The system was designed to diagnose infections and figure out what bacteria was the underlying cause.

Developed in the 1970s at Stanford University, the system relied on around 600 rules (Buchanan and Shortliffe 1984). Users would answer a series of questions. Based on these answers, the system would come up with a list of which bacteria could be the culprits. The results would be sorted in order of probability, along with a confidence score and explanations of how the conclusion was reached. The system would also recommend a course of treatment.

At a 69 percent accuracy rate, the system proved to be better at diagnostics than inexperienced doctors and on par with some experts (Yu, Victor, Fagan, Wraith, Clancey, Scott, Hannigan, Blum, Buchanan, and Cohen 1979).

The system's success relied on the fact that it had been fed a significant amount of data obtained by interviewing clinicians, diagnosticians, and other health care experts, who offered up their experience and expertise. It relied on an IF (condition) THEN (conclusion) methodology.

The system was never used in a clinical setting, though. First, it required a lot of computing power and would still take 30 minutes to come up with a diagnosis. In a real-world environment, this was far too long.

Legal and ethical concerns also came up, mainly connected to who would be liable if the system made a mistake, either in the diagnosis or the recommended treatment.

Despite it not being used in the real world, MYCIN still played an important role because many other rule-based programs in various fields were developed based on it.

Unfortunately, the development of AI experienced a series of setbacks. Otherwise, the field would have been far more advanced. These setbacks are popularly referred to as AI winters and are, basically, periods when the world lost interest in AI.

For example, in 1967, Marvin Minsky was confident that it would take no more than a generation to solve the problem of creating AI. However, by 1982, he was no longer so confident as he admitted it was one of the most difficult problems science had ever faced (Allen 2001).

The two main AI winters that set everything back were between 1974 and 1980 and from 1987 to 1993. The first winter was caused by several events that resulted in the belief that AI didn't have any real-world applications.

The first of these events was a report written by Sir James Lighthill, who believed that AI was a waste of time. He proposed that other sciences could achieve everything AI was doing and went on to imply that even the best algorithms set forth by the field of AI couldn't help with any problems in the real world (Lighthill 1973).

Funding for AI dried up, and, soon after, the 1969 Mansfield Amendment was passed in the United States. The amendment stated that DARPA was to only fund research with a clear objective and would result in technological solutions that the military could use. The shorter the timeframe for results, the better.

Using the Lighthill report as further proof that it would be a long while before AI generated anything useful for real-world applications, DARPA stopped funding anything AI-related. In fact, by 1974, it became practically impossible to find even the smallest amount of funding for any AI-based projects (National Research Council (U.S.) 1999).

The Speech Understanding Research program at Carnegie Mellon also contributed to the problem. DARPA's goal had been to obtain a system that pilots could use to control fighter planes. While the research team came up with a system that understood English, the words had to be said in a particular order. DARPA felt that they had been tricked as the system didn't even come close to what they wanted. So, in 1974, they canceled the grant (Crevier 1993; McCorduck 2004; National Research Council (U.S.) 1999).

By 1985, though, after the commercial success of various expert systems, interest in AI had been rekindled, and more than $1 billion was allocated to AI research. As a result, an entire industry developed to support the field of AI.

Machine Learning: Taking AI to a New Level

While classic AI research led to a wide range of beneficial discoveries and developments, it wasn't really AI as we see in science fiction, with machines that could truly think for themselves. More was required, which is where ML comes in.

Machine learning is what gets us closer to the human brain because it's meant to give a machine the ability to become more than its programming. To learn and improve beyond what we've taught it to do.

Therefore, ML is all about developing algorithms that can learn from the information they've been provided with, but that can also draw conclusions and make predictions pertaining to data they haven't yet analyzed.

Arthur Samuel, a pioneer in AI and computer gaming, first came up with the term of ML in 1959 while working at IBM. He stated that the goal of ML was to provide computers with the ability to learn without being programmed to do so (Samuel 1959).

Though one would assume that ML and classic AI would remain entangled, a rift occurred due to the focus on logical, knowledge-based approaches. ML became a separate field and gained significant traction in the 1990s. Rather than worrying about creating true AI, ML shifted toward developing solutions for more practical issues.

Machine learning remains a subfield of AI, but the approach it took was virtually the opposite of what had been done so far in AI research.

Classic AI worked with a rule-based, top-down approach, meaning that computers were provided with rules, which they had to follow to get to the desired result. The main concern with this approach was the significant amount of human input necessary.

Essentially, if you're the one designing the system, you have to think of every possible variable and eventuality that could arise and then create a set of rules for it. Unfortunately, since the system uses an IF/THEN approach, it doesn't handle uncertainty well.

This can create significant problems because very few things are quite that straightforward in life, especially if you're trying to create complicated software. IF (EVENT A) occurs, there's no guarantee that THEN (ACTION B) is the best solution or even the solution at all. For example, IF (RAINING) doesn't always lead to THEN (TAKE AN UMBRELLA). After all, you could always stay indoors and avoid the rain altogether.

That's not even the most significant issue. The real problem is that the only reason the system knows to provide this answer is that it has already been told what to do. That isn't in line with the ultimate goal of ML and AI, namely, to create a machine that can think for itself.

In contrast, ML starts at the other end, using a bottom-up, data-driven approach. In other words, in ML, data is used to teach the computer what to do. It's akin to the principle of teaching a man to fish rather than giving him the fish.

With ML, other than feeding the computer the data, there isn't much human input. Therefore, the machine can handle uncertainty more organically, which is the goal because the world consists more of probabilities than certainties.

With our rain/umbrella example, a machine would be fed with tons of data that it would analyze. It would see that, in some cases, when it's raining out, people will take umbrellas. In others, though, they will wait indoors until the rain has passed. It would look for patterns to differentiate when each event occurred, and it might discover that with lighter rain and warmer temperatures, people are more likely to brave the weather with an umbrella. However, if it's cold out and raining heavily, people are more likely to stay indoors. It picks up patterns, which it does by learning from the data it has been provided with.

Machine learning became very popular after the widespread adoption of the World Wide Web helped generate unprecedented amounts of data for the first time in human history. This, in combination with cheaper computing costs, has made ML the dominant approach in data science. These days, AI is practically synonymous with ML.

Statistics

Statistics is another core field of data science. It first came about in the 17th–18th centuries and was the first way people analyzed data in an organized, systematic fashion (Willcox 1938). It eventually led to the development of all the key aspects of modern data analysis, including regression, significant testing, summary statistics, and forecasting.

Traditionally, statistics dealt with small samples, mainly because of when it was developed. It's only relatively recently that we have become able to gather data remotely—at least when you consider how long the field of statistics has been around. When it was first developed, all data collection had to be done in person. Furthermore, everything had to be calculated by hand, so solving a model could take weeks.

The main difference between statistics and ML is that you must first validate and verify your assumptions with statistics. With ML, however, it's all about getting things done and asking questions later. While statistics offers a lot more transparency and interpretability, ML has led to amazing advances and performance.

However, ML does rely on computing, which means that models can be solved in minutes (usually far faster than that) instead of days. Therefore, multiple approaches can be attempted in far shorter time frames, leading to better performance and quicker progress.

Other Subfields of Data Science

Besides AI, ML, and statistics, data science also has other subfields, such as:

- Cybernetics, developed by Norbert Wiener in 1947;
- Artificial neural networks developed by McCulloch and Pitts in 1943;
- Computational intelligence developed in 1990;
- Data mining developed by Gregory Piatetsky-Shapiro in 1990 (McCulloch and Pitts 1943; Conway and Siegelman 2005; Russel and Norvig 2003; Samuel 1959; Piatetsky-Shapiro 1994).

The main problem for those not in the field is that all these terms have fluid definitions. Take two people with different research backgrounds, and they'll often give you different definitions for the same thing. While some conceptual differences exist, it often becomes difficult to tell unless you know who's doing the talking. Sometimes, it gets so complicated that even people who study these fields end up confused.

This is where the idea of data science came in. It simply made things a lot easier to explain. Saying a data scientist is someone who works with data is far simpler than trying to explain every field and subfield involved.

The essence of data science is that it allows us to take data and do useful things with it. While there are certainly all sorts of complex definitions available that cover tools and methodologies, at its core, data science is all about doing useful things with data.

A Dive Into ML for a Decision Maker

As we've seen, ML is vital to data science and can even be considered the next step up from classic AI. The main objective for ML is to enable computers to learn by being fed data rather than being explicitly programmed to do something.

Machine learning can be split into three major approaches: supervised learning, unsupervised learning, and reinforcement learning (Figure 2.1).

Supervised learning involves showing the machine what you want by providing examples. So, let's say you want it to organize a set of photos by separating them into images with humans and images containing vegetables. You'd provide an example of a photo with a human and one of a vegetable, making sure to label each appropriately. Then, the computer can sort the remaining images based on the labels you provided.

With unsupervised learning, you just provide the computer with the photos and allow it to organize them based on the different traits it can identify itself, without labels or human supervision.

Finally, with reinforcement learning, the system learns by making mistakes and receiving rewards when it gets things right. The computer analyzes the actions it took and the outcomes of those actions.

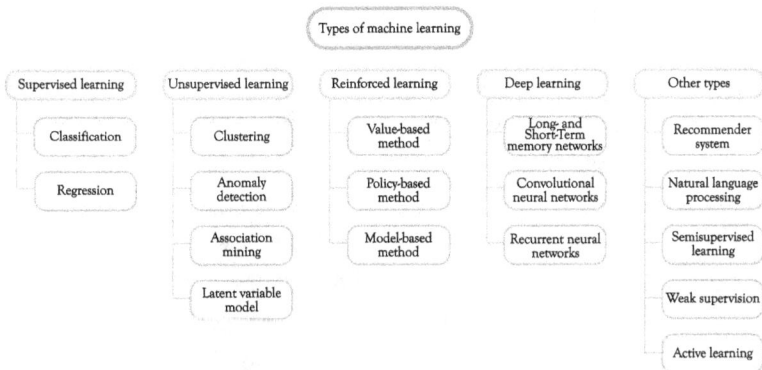

Figure 2.1 Types of machine learning

Supervised Learning

In supervised learning, algorithms learn by example with some form of supervision. It's almost like having a teacher supervising students, except that the students are algorithms in this case.

When you train such an algorithm, you provide training data consisting of inputs paired with the correct outputs. The machine will analyze the data in the training phase, looking for patterns that align with the desired outputs. So, you give the computer a bunch of photos of vegetables, and you tell it what each vegetable is. The computer analyzes this data to determine the pattern that leads to the correct conclusion. It will determine that an eggplant is oblong and dark purple, whereas a tomato is round and red.

Subsequently, after training has been completed, you can feed that algorithm new inputs, and it will classify the new data based on the training data it received. Therefore, it will classify oblong, dark purple objects as eggplants and round, red items as tomatoes.

The role of the supervisor is to correct the algorithm every time it makes a mistake. However, since the algorithm is constantly learning, it will eventually get to the point where it no longer makes mistakes.

It is, by far, the most popular flavor of ML. It is the primary technology used in task automation.

Supervised learning can be split into two categories: classification and regression.

Classification Models

Classification requires the algorithm to be provided with data that has been assigned to categories. The algorithm then takes inputs and assigns the categories based on the provided training data, like our previous example.

In real-world applications, the simplest example would be categorizing e-mails as spam or not spam, which is a binary classification problem.

The way it works is that the algorithm is provided with e-mails that are spam and e-mails that are not spam. It looks for the common features among each category. It will then use these patterns to classify unseen e-mails as either spam or not spam. As you already know, it doesn't always work right. However, every time you tell it that it's made a mistake, the algorithm learns. If you think about it, a decade ago, spam algorithms were wrong far more frequently than they are now. This is because every time someone marks an e-mail as not spam or vice versa, the algorithm learns. Considering that hundreds of millions of people use the same e-mail system (Gmail, for example), that's a lot of data for the algorithm to learn from.

Classification models can be used for other things, such as whether the value of a stock or commodity will rise or fall. They can also include more categories, so they don't have to be binary. For example, if you want to figure out who will win a talent competition with multiple contestants.

Regression Models

Regression, on the other hand, is a predictive statistical process. In this case, the algorithm tries to determine important relationships between dependent and independent variables. The goal is for the algorithm to be able to forecast actual numbers, such as sales and income.

In other words, instead of trying to figure out if the value of a commodity will rise or fall, we want to figure out what the price will be in seven days. Or, instead of determining whether a student will fail or pass a test, we want to know what grade they'll get. Maybe instead of attempting to figure out if the temperature this winter will be higher or lower, we want to know by how much. While these issues are related, they still represent different problems from their classification versions.

Most fields contain classification and regression problems. However, you must remember that these problems can be solved in multiple ways.

For example, let's say that you're a forex trader and you want to predict how the U.S. dollar will perform over the next few weeks so you can profit. You can use a classification model to figure out if it's going up or down, which will tell you whether to go short or long. However, you could also use a regression model for a more specific prediction, such as what price the EUR/USD will be trading at tomorrow.

In the first case, the situation is a little nebulous. While you might make a profit, the risk is far greater than if you were to use a regression model, which will give you more information to make an effective decision.

The idea is that each approach will give you different types of information that will impact performance and, ergo, the strategy you employ.

Unsupervised Learning

In unsupervised ML, an algorithm will infer patterns from data without the benefit of a targeted or labeled outcome. This type of learning cannot be applied to classification or regression problems because you don't know what the output might be, making it impossible to train the algorithm like normal.

In other words, unsupervised learning is all about the algorithm learning from data on its own and usually refers to clustering. This means that the training data you provide the algorithm only has inputs, without the desired outputs. Instead, the algorithm clusters the inputs based on the patterns it identifies. The system tries to find significant regularities that it can group. It involves no supervision.

With no guidance, this approach to ML can be challenging because the problems tend to be poorly defined. Unsupervised learning is effective, though, in helping to determine the data's underlying structure. Also, human interpretation is generally necessary, at the very least close to the end of the pipeline.

Unsupervised learning can discover patterns you wouldn't have otherwise known about. However, the reality is that it's not as effective as supervised learning. Another factor that makes supervised learning more applicable to practical problems is that, with unsupervised learning, you have no way of figuring out the accuracy of the results.

Unsupervised learning is generally best used when you don't have any information related to the desired outcome. One such example would be determining the target market of a completely new product. However, if you want to know more about your existing target market, then you're better off using supervised learning.

That doesn't mean unsupervised learning doesn't have its place. Some ways you can apply unsupervised learning are for clustering, anomaly detection, association mining, and latent variable models.

Clustering

With clustering, you can categorize the data into groups based on their similarity. It's not an approach that's widely used for applications such as customer segmentation, though, because it tends to overestimate how similar the groups are and doesn't see the data points as separate entities.

The biggest issue is that these types of problems are generally not well defined. For example, if you give an algorithm a series of images of various animals, the resulting clustering might not be relevant to your needs.

These images can be clustered in several ways, such as by color, type of animal, or habitat. None of these approaches are technically wrong, but some might be more useful than others.

The effectiveness of the result depends mainly on what your goal is. Therefore, it's important to have a well-defined goal and to experiment until you get it right. The good news is that if you test various algorithms, in the end, you will find one that works.

Anomaly Detection

Anomaly detection is useful for finding unusual information in your data. If something is unusual or anomalous in the data set, these algorithms will find it.

These algorithms have a wide range of real-world applications, especially for things like spotting fraudulent transactions. They can also be used to spot spikes in sales of various products but are just as helpful in detecting hackers.

Association Mining

Association mining is often used for basket analysis because it effectively identifies items that appear together frequently in your data. It's often used to help determine correlations in transactional, sales, and even medical data.

Latent Variable Models

Latent variable models are used to make the data easier to analyze and come in during the preprocessing phase. These models are effective for doing things such as lowering the number of features in a set of data, also known as dimensionality reduction, or even splitting the data up into multiple components.

With dimensionality reduction, the goal is to group together large numbers of variables into a lower number of factors, making the data easier to interpret. One of the most widely used techniques is factor analysis.

An example is the Big Five Personality Inventory, which was developed by gathering data from a large number of people and applying factor analysis to group the answers into five overall factors. Based on the Big Five personality theory, our personalities can be categorized as:

- Extraversion
- Agreeableness
- Conscientiousness
- Neuroticism
- Openness to experience

However, each of these major factors is made up of a wide range of variables. For example, an extroverted personality is characterized by friendliness, cheerfulness, assertiveness, and much more.

Dimensionality reduction can be applied to many other problems, including user demographics and customer data.

Reinforcement Learning

Many experts believe reinforcement learning to be one of the keys to unlocking real AI because of the vast potential it holds. Moreover, it is growing at an accelerated pace and producing a wide range of algorithms for various applications.

Reinforcement learning is based on a punishment/reward system. It's a little like training your pet pooch. If you want to teach Fido to sit on command, you'll give him the command, show him what you want, and reward him with a treat. For a while, you continue to reward him every time he gets it right to reinforce the behavior.

When Fido doesn't listen to you, you usually have to repeat what you want until he does it and then reward him. Not receiving a reward is generally "punishment" enough for him to get that he's done wrong.

With an algorithm, things work slightly differently, but in essence, they are the same. For example, let's consider a robot learning to walk. If the step it takes is too long, it loses its balance and tips over. That's the punishment. So, it will keep changing the length of its step until it can move without falling over, which is the reward.

Or consider the same robot attempting to navigate a maze. Things are a little more complex here because it's not just an immediate solution. In the previous example, adjusting the length of the step will yield immediate results. With a maze, the first few steps might be right, until it reaches a dead-end and has to backtrack until it finds open space.

You might be wondering what the point is. Well, consider some real-world applications. Reinforcement learning is used for such things as driverless cars, robot vacuum cleaners, and more. Without reinforcement learning, your vacuum cleaner would keep slamming into the same obstacle instead of backing up to move around it.

Reinforcement learning is the closest thing to learning like a human. Consider that any skill you learn and develop is based on experience. Therefore, the more you practice, the better you get. However, it all boils down to reward/punishment. You've learned by discovering what works and what doesn't.

Consider chess. The more you play, the better you get. That's because you amass more and more experience on what works and what doesn't in different situations.

Reinforcement learning for machines works much the same way, which is why so many consider it to have so much potential. It allows for the resolution of very complex problems in a variety of environments.

Deep Learning

Deep learning studies neural networks that have multiple layers, also known as deep neural networks. A neural network is made up of neurons and the pathways that connect them, a bit like a connect-the-dots picture. The human brain is the most powerful computer that exists, so it makes sense for us to model artificial computers on something that already works so well.

In deep learning, artificial neural networks are used to help machines learn more quickly, more effectively, and at far greater volumes. It has been used to solve various problems that were believed to be unsolvable, such as natural language processing (NLP), speech recognition, and computer vision.

At a very basic level, the way it works is that the input is generated from observation, which is then added to a layer. That layer generates an output, which becomes the input for the following layers until you get to the final output.

For example, when you look at a picture of an eggplant, you know it's an eggplant. But how do you know it's an eggplant and not an airplane or a basketball?

Your eyes see a specific shape and a specific color, and, based on experience, it translates those inputs into an abstract concept you understand. All this information is filtered from your eyes through multiple layers until it becomes an eggplant rather than an airplane.

Software applications such as Siri, Cortana, or Dragon Naturally Speaking can all understand you because of deep learning. It's also what allows these applications to learn and improve the more they interact with you.

This also applies to image or song recognition. Want to find out what a specific song is? Just get your app to listen to it, and it will be able to identify it. Likewise, want to find a particular item you can see in the real world? Take a photo of it, and the app will find it for you online.

Deep learning can also be used to generate language. OpenAI's GPT-3 is a very impressive model that can create articles so realistic that it is practically impossible to figure out a machine writes them.

Another application for deep learning is that it has given computers the ability to identify different subjects in an image, such as being able to tell that chickens, horses, cats, and humans are different things.

It's also being used in things like graphic design with plugins and apps that can remove backgrounds from photos while maintaining the full integrity of the subject. If you've ever tried to remove a background, you know how difficult it can be.

If it's not something you've attempted, then trust us when we say that, before deep learning enabled the creation of these apps, you needed a lot of time and patience. Even then, you still weren't guaranteed to get a result as good as these apps can offer in a fraction of the time.

It's a bit like the difference between hand painting one of those eggs with highly complex designs and painting your bedroom wall with a spray gun.

In conclusion, deep learning has allowed us to achieve some incredible things with machines and will continue to do so. Some believe that it might lead us to true AI, whereas others say that progress has plateaued. The big question for AI researchers is: what comes after deep learning? Only time will tell.

Other Types of ML

Quite a few other types of ML exist, including recommender systems, NLP, active learning, semisupervised learning, and weak supervision.

Recommender systems are designed to predict user interest and make recommendations accordingly. These are some of the most powerful ML systems used by retailers online to boost sales (Rodriguez 2018).

Consider Amazon, which has an excellent recommender system. Every time you log in, Amazon will recommend products or books they think you might like based on previous purchases and visits.

Spotify or Netflix use similar data to make recommendations in terms of the content you might enjoy. For example, if you watch a lot of action movies and crime dramas, then Netflix will recommend similar films and TV shows.

In ML, **Natural Language Processing** and text analytics involve the use of algorithms and AI to understand text, which can range from Facebook comments and online reviews to e-mails and regulatory documents (Barba 2020).

Active learning refers to the process of prioritizing data that must be labeled, so it has the highest impact on training a supervised model (Solaguren-Beascoa 2020).

Semisupervised learning combines supervised and unsupervised ML methods so that an algorithm learns from data sets that include labeled and unlabeled data ("Semi-Supervised Machine Learning" n.d.).

Weak supervision or weakly supervised learning comprises a variety of approaches, including:

- Inexact supervision, where the training data is provided with only coarse-grained labels;
- Incomplete supervision that features data sets with only one subset that has labels;
- Inaccurate supervision, where the labels aren't always ground truth (Zhou 2018).

For Decision Makers: How to Use Machine Learning

Machine learning really shines in cases where automation or prediction are needed. Irrespective of the actual form of ML being used in most cases, it is applied to the following cases:

1. Humans are performing a repetitive task, which also allows them to label data. The labeled data can then be used to train a ML model to replace the human. The most prominent example of this is computer vision and applications such as face recognition or recognizing certain entities in a photo (e.g., humans vs animals).

2. Predicting something about the future or an unknown quantity: credit scoring, spam detection, forecasting, customer churn all are viable applications of ML.

Understanding when and how to apply ML is a skill that takes a long time to master. However, a decision maker can just use the aforementioned heuristics to get a feeling of when they could use it. What is more important from a decision maker's perspective is making sure that there is a data strategy in place that can facilitate the use of ML. This is covered in the next chapter.

A Brief Intro to Statistics for the Decision Maker

Statistics is one of the core fields of data science. It was the first discipline to deal with data collection and analysis in a systematic way. In this section we will provide a brief overview of that area, as it can help us better understand the domain of data science.

Statistics is the study of how to collect, organize, analyze, and interpret numerical information and data. It encompasses both the science of uncertainty and the technology of extracting information from data.

It is a vital tool for any data scientist and is used to help us make decisions. This field employs a variety of methodologies that enable data scientists to do a variety of things, including:

- Design experiments and interpret results to improve product decision making;
- Develop models to predict signals;
- Mold data into insights;
- Understand a wide range of variables, including engagement, conversions, retention, leads, and more;
- Make intelligent estimations;
- Use data to tell the story.

From a decision maker's perspective, statistics is important to understand, and also to get a good understanding of how they fit into the whole narrative of data science. While the discipline of statistics cannot be considered an emerging field (since it has been around for more than 200 years), it has found new uses in the era of big data.

Many data science applications, which could be considered emerging tech, are based on simple applications of statistics. Therefore, getting a good understanding of the basic uses of statistics can help put things into perspective as to how technologies and methodologies evolve and adapt as technology advances.

A Little History About Statistics

Statistics is a branch of mathematics dating back to approximately the 18th century. It was humanity's first attempt to analyze data systematically and is at the base of modern data analysis. It led to the development of summary statistics, regression classification, significant testing, forecasting, and more. Some prominent individuals in this field include Ronald Fisher, Karl Pearson (and his son Egon Pearson), and Jerzy Neyman.

Statistics is different from other data analysis fields because it focuses more on the theoretical soundness of the models and has traditionally dealt with smaller samples. This is mainly due to historical reasons because data had to be collected in person until relatively recently. It's only since the advent of the Internet that we can collect data remotely, allowing for much larger sample sizes.

As you can imagine, collecting data in person was not only expensive but also time-consuming, which meant that small sample sizes were the norm. Furthermore, until computers became part of our lives, calculations had to be done manually. While the results were extrapolated to the entire population using a margin of error, those calculations still took time. Today, solving a model might take seconds, but in the 18th century, it would've taken days or weeks.

There's also a different mentality when it comes to statistics. As this field is rooted in math, it is very strict on model assumptions and development. These assumptions must be validated and verified before you can do anything else. On the other hand, in ML, the goal is to achieve the objective and ask questions later.

One crucial difference between ML and statistics, for example, is that ML has led to impressive performance, even though statistics is far more transparent and has a higher degree of interpretability. The thing is that the high-level performance ML offers means that we've been able to achieve things that were previously thought impossible.

While some statisticians are completely against ML because of the reduced level of transparency and lack of theory, the fact is that statistics and ML work hand-in-hand. They are also both tools the data scientist can and should use depending on the situation. In other words, if you want interpretability, then you should turn to statistics. On the other hand, if you're looking for performance and predictive power, then ML is the way to go.

A Short Intro to Statistics

Statistics can be split into two branches: descriptive and inferential statistics.

Descriptive statistics is what most people consider statistics to be. It involves collecting data, using summary metrics such as the name and data visualization.

On the other hand, inferential statistics is what most people in the field consider to be statistics. It involves more advanced concepts such as sampling and inferring values of the population parameters.

Descriptive Statistics

Descriptive statistics involves organizing, summarizing, and presenting data so everyone can understand and make use of it. To do this, there are two sets of methods, namely numerical methods to describe data and graphical methods for data presentation ("Understanding Descriptive and Inferential Statistics | Laerd Statistics" n.d.).

Numerical methods encompass metrics not only for data location, such as the mean, median, and mode but also measures of data variability, such as variance and standard deviation.

Graphical methods for data representation include bar charts, histograms, pie charts, and more.

Many analytics products in the market, such as Tableaux or other dashboards, are usually focused on descriptive statistics. While descriptive statistics are simple, they can be very effective and easily understood by anyone.

Inferential Statistics

Inferential statistics represents the majority of the field because that's where the work is really done, while descriptive statistics represents a tiny fraction.

Inferential statistics comprises a group of methods you can use to draw conclusions or inferences about the traits of a whole population based on sample data.

In essence, inferential statistics allows you to quantify uncertainty. So, for example, let's say that you want to figure out something about a group of people. It could be something like the average age of the population.

If you were dealing with a small population, say maybe a few hundred people, then you could measure everyone's age and calculate the average. However, when you try to do that for an entire country, for example, that might have a population of 20 million people, it will be practically impossible. Well, at least unfeasible from a cost and effort viewpoint.

So, if studying every individual is impractical, there must be an alternative. That's where inferential statistics comes in. It involves taking a sample of the population you are attempting to study and expressing uncertainty through probability distribution. You're essentially turning uncertainty into a quantifiable metric, which then allows you to run calculations. That is what permits statistical modeling and hypothesis testing.

What you do is take a sample of a thousand people, which covers as wide a demographic as possible and then extrapolate their average age to the entire population of 20 million. While demographic conformity is not absolutely necessary, it does lead to more accurate results.

For example, consider deaths caused by the coronavirus. There were many conversations over the first few months of the pandemic about the actual mortality rate of the disease. Many disagreements arose between statisticians. At least some of those deaths attributed to COVID-19 were caused by other conditions. Still, at the same time, some covid-related deaths, especially before tests became available, were attributed to other illnesses. This is a classic problem of inferential statistics: trying to decipher the value of an underlying variable, given a sample.

Another interesting inferential issue around COVID-19-related deaths is related to definitions and attribution. Let's say someone had severe underlying conditions and would probably die within the next month. If this person died and then tested positive for COVID-19, was the illness the cause of death or the underlying conditions?

The topic of attribution raises more of a philosophical discussion and is encountered in many health-related discussions. For example, who is the true culprit of the obesity epidemic? The companies selling unhealthy food, the advertisers, or the people buying it? While many people will have strong opinions on the subject, it is difficult to attribute this phenomenon to a single factor completely. This is where inferential statistics can help provide more clarity by quantifying each factors' contribution.

The Benefits of Statistics

All this might sound very interesting, but you're probably wondering how statistics can help you in business as a decision maker.

First, you're probably already using descriptive statistics in some shape or form. Profit and loss forecasts are just one example of using statistics in a business setting.

Inferential statistics, on the other hand, can be used to answer specific questions regarding the importance of a variable. It can also answer questions about differences in population.

The main things you'll be using inferential statistics for are hypothesis testing and statistical modeling. While forecasting is another beneficial area, it is somewhat more technical, and it can often be achieved using ML more easily than through statistics.

Hypothesis testing is generally used for finding out the value of a population parameter or making comparisons.

Working out the value of a population basically means that you are looking to determine the specific value, such as average height, average income, and average age. Comparisons involve analyzing the differences and/or similarities among parameters. One example would be exploring differences based on gender. So, you would look at whether men earn more or less money in a specific job than women.

In business, especially online, you might have already heard of A/B testing, which is a form of comparison. So, when you test two calls-to-action against each other to determine which generates the highest conversion rate, you are conducting a comparison-based hypothesis test.

Statistical modeling is what you use when you want to figure out if one variable affects another.

So, let's say you've conducted your comparison-based hypothesis test on your calls-to-action to determine which is more effective at achieving conversions. You've established which one is more successful, but you also want to learn what other variables could be affecting your conversion rate. To do so, you would use statistical modeling.

Essentially, you plug in your variables into the model and may discover that everything, from the button's position on the page and the color of the text to the headline and content, affects conversion rates. You can also determine to what degree these variables affect conversion rates. For example, you might find that the headline and call-to-action play only a small part in why people are converting and that the main draw is the offer itself.

Applications of Statistics in Business and Economics

In today's digital world, we have vast amounts of statistical data available to us at our fingertips. The most effective business leaders and decision makers are aware of the value of this data and can use it effectively. Here are some of the applications of statistics in business:

Accounting

Accounting companies often use statistical sampling methods when they conduct audits for clients. For example, let's say that an accounting company wants to figure out if the accounts receivable on the client's balance sheet accurately represents the total amount of accounts receivable (Dilip n.d.).

Large corporations often have significant numbers of individual accounts receivable, which makes it far too time-consuming and expensive to validate each entry. Thus, the audit team will often select a sample of those accounts and, after reviewing and validating them, the auditors will conclude whether the amount on the balance sheet is accurate or not.

Finance

Financial analysis involves the use of a lot of statistical information to help investors make decisions. For example, Forex trading relies on the analysis of financial data, including historical price movement, a country's economic data, and much more. It also involves using a wide range of indicators that are calculated using statistical information, such as the moving average.

The same applies to stocks, where investors make decisions on which stock to invest in based on variables such as price/earnings ratios and dividend yields. Some might even conduct a comparison between the market average and the results of an individual stock.

Marketing

Statistics is also highly useful in marketing. Electronic scanners at retail checkout counters collect data for various marketing research applications. AC Nielsen, an information supplier, purchases this data from grocery stores, then processes it and sells statistical summaries to manufacturers and distributors, among others.

Companies will spend a lot of money to obtain this kind of data because it can be used to determine production necessities and even assist in developing new products.

Production

Quality control is an essential application of statistics in manufacturing. Various statistical quality control charts are used to monitor the output of the manufacturing process, such as an x-bar chart, which can be used to monitor average output.

For example, let's say that a machine fills containers with 1.5 ounces of cream. Sporadically, an employee will select a sample of containers and calculate the average number of ounces in the sample. This average value is then plotted on an x-bar chart.

A plotted value above the upper control limit indicates that the machine is overfilling the containers, whereas a plotted value below the lower control limit indicates underfilling. The process continues as long as the plotted value falls between the upper and lower control limits. Otherwise, adjustments are made to ensure the average is where it should be.

Economics

Economists frequently predict the future of the economy or certain aspects of it. They use a variety of statistical information to make these predictions, such as forecasting GDP, inflation rates, and more. However, these predictions are often made using ML.

Information Systems

Information systems administrators handle the daily operations of the company's computer networks. They use various statistical information to assess performance and make adjustments to ensure that the system is functioning optimally.

The Pitfalls of Statistics

One of the biggest problems with statistics is that people tend to trust them blindly simply because they appear to be facts. After all, when someone presents you with information, and it's backed by what looks like accurate data in the form of numbers, ratios, percentages, graphs, charts, and so on, you're far more likely to believe what you're being told.

However, it is very easy to use statistics to lie to people. While it's not always a matter of bad intentions, even human error can lead to skewed results, which can cause problems.

Therefore, it's essential that you understand how statistics can be used to distort facts. This way, you will be more aware and less likely to make poor decisions because you've been misled.

Here are some of the ways in which you can be lied to using statistics:

Lying Using Charts

One way statistics can be used to mislead an audience is by lying to people using charts that contain spurious correlations. They seem to make sense at first glance but have no connection one to another.

For example, here is one chart that correlates the divorce rate in Maine with the per capita consumption of margarine (Figure 2.2).

Here's another chart that attempts to correlate worldwide noncommercial space launches with sociology doctorates awarded in the United States (Figure 2.3). Now, these might seem like interesting statistics and, separately, they certainly are. However, when you try to establish a correlation between these facts, it's a bit ridiculous.

For example, the first chart seems to imply that as divorce rates decline in Maine, so too does the consumption of margarine. Some enterprising individuals might attempt to convince you that margarine has affected the divorce rate, and the less margarine people eat, the less likely they are to get a divorce.

The second chart seems to imply that an increase in sociology doctorates has led to a rise in the number of worldwide noncommercial space launches. Now, you might scoff and say that it's quite obvious there are no correlations between these variables. After all, how can the

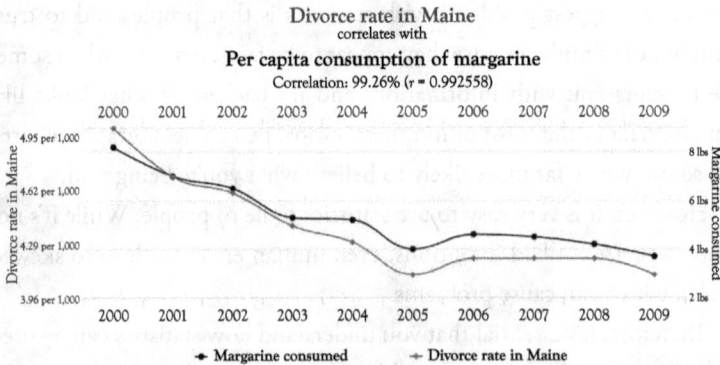

Figure 2.2 Divorce rate in Maine

Sources: National vital statistics reports and U.S. department of agriculture

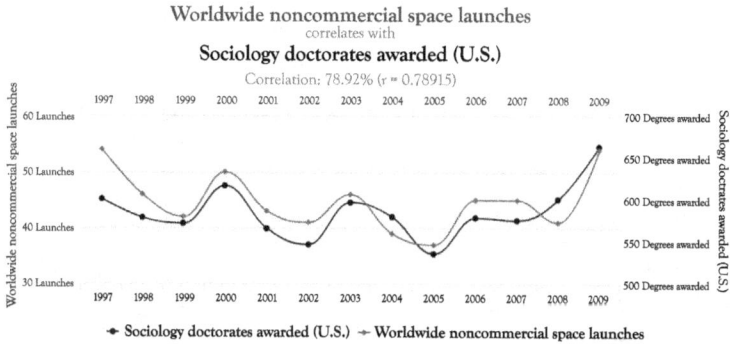

Figure 2.3 *Worldwide noncommercial space launches*

Source: Federal aviation administration and national science foundation

number of sociology doctorates awarded in the United States affect space launches? However, what happens is that people use variables that might seem to have a tangential connection to each other to attempt to convince you that a spurious correlation is fact.

A spurious correlation means that someone is trying to correlate two variables that don't really have an underlying theory that holds up to scrutiny. They are simply comparing two variables that aren't connected. Furthermore, it's important to remember that correlation doesn't necessarily imply causation.

For example, the consumption of margarine is in no way related to the number of divorces in Maine. After all, it's not like a spread can have such an impact on people's relationships. You might go so far as to say that an argument over margarine led to a divorce. However, if people are arguing over margarine so much that they end up divorcing, there are many other underlying issues, and margarine is only an excuse rather than a cause.

However, if we were to attempt to correlate the consumption of margarine and income in the margarine industry, then the correlation would make sense because the two are connected.

In some charts, people can be tricked even more because things like reversing the X- and Y-axis can lead to mistaken conclusions. For example, suppose the numbers along the X-axis decrease while those on the Y-axis increase. In that case, this will lead to an erroneous visual representation, which is another way to attempt to force a correlation.

So, just remember that even if there might seem to be a significant correlation between two variables, that doesn't actually mean there is a relationship between the two.

Another way you can be lied to with charts is by using different types of scales in the same chart. For example, you can use different scales to make items seem as if they're closer to each other.

Another way to lie is to change the scale. If you close in on the scale, a variable's evolution might seem choppy. However, when you zoom out, it looks far more stable.

For example, if you take a snapshot of last year's performance of the Dow Jones industrial index (simply google "Dow Jones chart") you will see that growth has stalled (Figure 2.4). But if you look at a multidecade chart, you will see that the index has been rising over the long run (Figure 2.5). An analyst who focuses on recent developments might get worried, while someone focused more on the long run can be reassured that the economy will simply keep growing. Graph interpretation can be quite subjective at times, and this is why a decision maker must always be skeptical and critical of any graph interpretations.

Embellishing With Descriptive Statistics

Descriptive statistics can also be used to mislead people, and one way to do so quite easily is through measures of centrality and summary metrics.

You have three main measures of centrality: the median, the mode, and the mean.

The mean represents the average of a set of numbers, which is basically where you add all the numbers together and divide the result by the number of variables you added together. The median is the central value in a list of numbers, and the mode is the value that shows up most frequently in a list.

If a distribution is symmetrical, these three values will fall on the same point. However, if the distribution is positively skewed, the mean will be lighter than the median, and the median will be lighter than the mode. If the distribution is negatively skewed, then the opposite happens.

It's important to note this because most distributions in life aren't symmetrical. For example, let's say that a company pays its CEO $300,000 per year, while the rest of the 10 employees earn $50,000 per year each.

Figure 2.4 Dow Jones industrial index for 2020

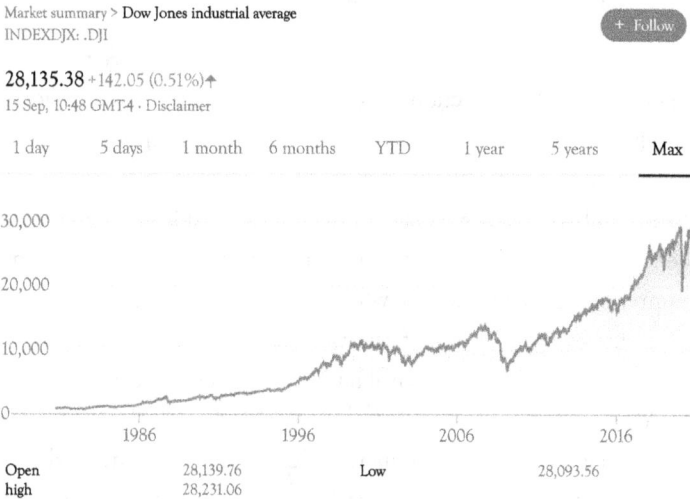

Figure 2.5 Dow Jones industrial index long-term trend

Depending on what you want to achieve, you can present different numbers. In this case, the median might be $50,000 per year, but the mean is $72,000 per year.

A company could advertise the mean figure, which would make people think that that's what they could earn, but the company is unwilling to pay more than $50,000 per year for anybody other than the CEO.

This way, they could trick potential employees into accepting a job because they believe they will eventually earn $72,000, when in fact, they'll never receive more than $50,000. It might seem underhanded—it is, in case you were wondering—but not as unusual as you might think.

Sampling Biases.   Sampling biases can also lead to less than accurate data that can cause problems in the decision-making process. While there are quite a few different sampling biases, we will be looking at five: the selection bias, the area bias, the self-selection bias, the leading question bias, and social desirability bias, as they are the most common in business.

Two very famous cases of sampling bias are the forecasting of the Brexit vote in Britain and the 2016 presidential election in the United States. The forecasters in both cases got it completely wrong, because of bias that got introduced into the sample and completely invalidated most statistical models that were used (Kampakis 2016).

Selection Bias.   The selection bias is the most significant. In fact, the other types of bias can actually be seen as related or even as subcategories of selection bias.

Selection bias occurs when the sample being used is not representative of the whole. Something is going on that ensures the subjects or items in the sample are special somehow, while other subjects are left out.

One interesting example of selection bias is the attempt of the U.S. government to increase the survival rate of U.S. aircraft during the Second World War.

The initial attempt was conducted after investigators analyzed planes that had survived. The recommendation was to add more armor to the areas that had received the most amount of damage. When the armor was mounted, instead of leading to a higher rate of survivability, the exact opposite happened. The extra armor made the planes heavier, slower, and far less agile, making it easier for the enemy to destroy them. Furthermore, the aircraft that survived still had significant amounts of damage in the same areas.

The government turned to Abraham Wald, who was a statistician. He realized that selection bias was taking place. In other words, instead of looking at what was important, the investigators made their decisions based on planes that had survived the damage they received. That's when Wald concluded that the areas that required protection were actually the areas that were sensitive and hadn't been damaged. Once those areas were reinforced, survivability increased (Mangel and Samaniego 1984).

This is an interesting way that you can use statistics without even conducting any significant analysis. Wald had to understand that selection bias was taking place, which allowed them to fix the problem.

Area Bias.   Area bias refers to attempting to generalize results from one area to another. This poses many problems, especially when you're trying to cross cultures.

For example, if you conduct marketing research in the United States, and you attempt to apply the results to another area, such as the Middle East, you're going to have a big surprise. The cultural, financial, lingual, and many other differences will have a significant impact, basically making those results null and void.

Self-Selection Bias.   Self-selection bias refers to the increased likelihood of a person deciding to participate in a study because of traits they already have.

For example, if you conduct a study on using makeup, you are more likely to get people participating in the survey who use makeup frequently than those who don't at all or do so rarely.

The problem is that this leads to a nonrepresentative sample. Of course, this depends on what you're attempting to achieve. However, if you want the sample to be truly representative, you need to talk to people who use makeup and who don't use makeup or use it rarely.

Leading Questions Bias.   A very easy way to get the answers you want rather than the truth is to use leading questions in your questionnaires.

For example, if you ask someone if they believe teachers aren't paid enough and the answers you provide them are:

  (a) Yes, they should earn more;
  (b) No, they should not earn more;
  (c) No opinion.

   Most people will say A; teachers should definitely be paid more. This is because people want to be nice and provide what seem like socially acceptable answers. Plus, the way the question was phrased only really gives them one option.

Social Desirability Bias.   Social desirability bias occurs when people want to paint themselves in a better light, which is almost always. So, if you pose questions about social desirability issues, your data will be skewed because nobody wants to admit they don't fall in line with societal expectations. So, for example, if you ask someone how frequently they donate to charity, or how often they recycle, or how much food they throw away, you are unlikely to receive accurate answers.

   If someone tells you that they only throw out 3 percent of the food they buy, they are probably not telling the truth since throwing away food is not exactly considered socially acceptable as it's a massive waste. So, they will provide an answer they feel is more socially acceptable instead of the truth.

Lying With Inferential Statistics

Some believe that it's impossible to lie with inferential statistics. Unfortunately, that's not exactly accurate. It might be challenging to lie with inferential statistics, but it can still be done.

   This takes place a lot in research. When testing a hypothesis, you'll get a p-value. This value needs to be below a certain threshold for the tests to have statistical significance. Generally speaking, this threshold is 0.05.

   A theory says that a significant number of research papers have p-values that are unusually close to 0.05. In other words, the results of these papers seem significant, but only by a tiny margin, because the value of p is just below 0.05, allowing them to meet the condition of the statistical significance.

The theory in question says that this is being done on purpose. Academia is a very competitive environment, and people have to publish papers, or they'll end up without a job. So, people are basically under pressure to make the results look as if they are statistically significant. One way to achieve this is by conducting multiple experiments until you get the results you want.

Another way to do this is by massaging the data. However, in other cases, you can find research where the results are significant, but this is only because the model assumptions aren't being met and not because the researcher intended to deceive.

Case Studies and Examples

Here are some examples where data science can make a significant impact on business.

Preventive Maintenance Becomes Predictive Maintenance

Preventive maintenance is a key aspect of business for many firms across a wide range of industries because of the reduction of unplanned downtime. The latter can negatively affect the bottom line, which is why preventive maintenance is so valuable.

Like with any other aspect of business, improving maintenance efficiency is a big priority for many firms, especially those that rely on a lot of expensive machinery. Companies operating in industries such as manufacturing, shipping, oil and gas, rail, and freight can all benefit.

The goal of regular maintenance is to minimize failures, maximize the life of a machine, and ensure optimal performance and efficient operation.

The most common approach is for firms to use a maintenance schedule based on recommendations made by the manufacturer of the equipment or vehicles. It's just like with your car, where the manufacturer recommends you change the oil after 10,000 miles, for example.

This isn't a bad approach at all. It's certainly better than guessing or waiting for something to break down. However, it isn't ideal because failures still happen. The fact is that no one can plan for every situation and predict every issue.

For example, a manufacturer might recommend that you change fuel filters every 5,000 hours of operation, but that's in ideal operating conditions. If the diesel hasn't been the best quality or the machine is operating in very dusty or sandy conditions, the change will need to come sooner unless you want a lot of other problems to occur.

Avoiding unplanned downtime due to failures and breakdowns is essential because this downtime can be very expensive. It leads to a significant loss of revenue through lost output and reduced productivity.

The better alternative is planned downtime because you can plan to conduct maintenance at a time when the machine being inoperable will cause the least amount of problems. The key is figuring out when that is.

Many firms are turning to data and predictive analytics to solve their issues with maintenance scheduling (Kampakis 2020a).

In manufacturing, for example, the sensors on a production line can collect almost any information you need. You can then store and analyze the data. Algorithms can then use the data to determine when a failure might occur. This process is referred to as predictive maintenance.

The predictive maintenance algorithms being used at the moment are usually based on ML, so their accuracy improves as they get better at identifying situations when failures are possible.

Furthermore, the whole process can be automated, which means that predictive analytics can work out when maintenance is necessary to avoid failure. It can also determine the best time for maintenance to occur to ensure it is the least disruptive, based on a variety of factors such as demand.

Predictive maintenance offers significant boosts in productivity, improves customer service, reduces costs, and improves profits. As Google trends show, it has become very popular and will continue to increase in popularity as more firms understand the benefits.

Using AI and Data Science to Fight COVID-19

Owing to the novel coronavirus dubbed COVID-19, the world is facing a crisis that no one thought could occur in the modern world. At the time of this writing, the death toll has almost reached one million on a global scale with a total of 31.4 million cases of infection, and the crisis is still ongoing, with many experts warning of a second wave of mass infections.

Many organizations have turned to AI and data science to help in this time of crisis (Kampakis 2020b). The White House and the Allen Institute for AI have released a database of 29,000 research articles on the coronavirus family. These articles have been modified to ensure they are machine-readable by NLP libraries.

Using AI, researchers hope they will be able to generate new insights from all the work that's already been done into understanding this virus family.

The data set has also been put up as a Kaggle challenge to take advantage of crowdsourcing to come up with new insights and possible solutions.

AI can also assist in detecting people who are very vulnerable to infection and developing severe complications from the virus. Medical Home Network uses such a system to first address those patients who are most in need of medical care.

AI can also help to create vaccines. A team from Australia's Flinders University designed an AI that managed to develop a drug on its own for the first time. While the technology is still in its infancy and not much help fighting COVID-19, it could be vital for a future pandemic.

AI can also help to reduce the strain on health care networks, with chatbots replacing doctors to answer simple questions. For example, Ask-Sophie helps patients determine whether they have a common cold or COVID-19 ("Check Your Symptoms | Medicare" n.d.).

Traditional predictive analytics can also help forecast the future. Researchers in Israel, for example, are relying on AI to predict when the next breakout might occur, so they are in a better position to prevent it. The Israelis don't have a large number of tests available, so they need to be careful how they use them. They are, therefore, handing out questionnaires daily and relying on data science to work out which clusters of people could be infected.

Hiring the Right Person

As it has become clear by now, data science is a big and convoluted field, primarily because it is an aggregation of different scientific disciplines. This means that there are many different types of data scientists, and hiring one can be a fairly complicated process, as backgrounds can vary. A ML specialist might have a very different skillset from a pure statistician. We are looking into the topic of hiring and managing data scientists in Chapter 4 later on.

Key Takeaways

- Data science is a term that aggregates many different fields. The core ones being AI, ML, and statistics.
- The most popular types of ML are supervised and unsupervised learning. There are other subtypes, such as active learning and recommender systems, which can be useful for certain types of businesses.
- Statistics is broken down into descriptive and inferential statistics. The most interesting applications (like statistical modeling) fall within the spectrum of inferential statistics.
- When working with statistical methods it's important to try and avoid potential biases that might creep into the data.
- Hiring and managing a data scientist is not always easy, because there are data scientists of many different backgrounds.

CHAPTER 3

What Is a Data Strategy?

Now that we have covered a high-level overview of data science, we move on to talk about data strategy. This is key for any business that wants to generate value from its data, and it is just as important as hiring the right person.

There are many varying definitions of a data strategy on the Internet, but a good definition would be the following:

> *A data strategy is a **living** document that defines how the business is setting itself up, both from a technical and organizational perspective, to proactively manage and leverage data towards the long-term business strategy.*

This definition is made up of several key components:

A data strategy is a living document … —A data strategy should not be a document that takes months to develop and then is put to one side, gathering dust for no one to read again. By all means, the data strategy can be a document, a presentation, or whatever other medium you choose, but above all, it should be a living document—meaning that it is constantly updated and refreshed as the business evolves.

… defines how the business is setting itself up, both from a technical and organizational perspective… —A good data strategy should ideally cover both the engineering and infrastructure approach and how you plan to structure the organization and teams to make the most of your data.

… to proactively manage and leverage data … —By creating a data strategy, you make sure that you take proactive measures to make the business as resilient as possible and give it as much of a competitive advantage as early as possible.

… toward the long-term business strategy—Last but certainly not the least, a data strategy should not exist in isolation from the rest of the

business. Instead, a good data strategy will have the business strategy as its north star, and all of the plans should stem from this.

Why Is a Data Strategy Important?

Have you ever wondered what happens every minute on the Internet? Google processes 3.8 million search queries, 4.5 million videos are watched on YouTube, 188 million e-mails are sent, and approximately 700,000 hours are watched on Netflix. As our lives have become increasingly digital, the interactions we have with products and services can be recorded and observed like never before.

What do Nike, L'Oreal, Vodafone, and Transport for London have in common? On the face of it, all of these businesses operate in different markets and offer completely different products. However, they are all data-driven businesses.

In recent decades, data has transformed from being a side effect of products to one of the most valuable assets in a business. Data is multifaceted in the way it can add value. Still, one can broadly categorize the areas where data adds value as operational improvements, customer insights, and data as a product.

1. Operational Improvements:
   - Data can improve or even fully automate processes within our businesses. For example, Verizon uses data to triage customer service calls and thus optimize their call centers. In addition, data-rich business areas such as supply chain logistics are prime targets to be automated.
   - Another example of this is how Netflix has invested large sums into optimizing the production process so they can create original content at scale (Kumar, Misra, Walraven, Sharan, Azarnoush, Chen, and Govind 2018).
2. Customer Insights:
   - Many of today's most popular services use data as a tool to deliver a better product experience for the customer. For example, LinkedIn uses your past interactions to recommend posts you may be interested in. Spotify's Discover Weekly is another

fantastic example of using data and ML to generate recommendations and increase user engagement.

3. Data as a Product:

- Finally, data in and of itself can add immense value to the business as a new revenue stream. Typically, this area of value will only be relevant once a company has scaled to thousands of users and is generating significant amounts of data, but it should not be underestimated.

- Owning large amounts of user data can greatly increase the value of a company in the eyes of an acquirer. IBM acquired Weather Underground as part of a deal that was valued at approximately $2 billion by *The Wall Street Journal*, demonstrating the value of the data they possessed to IBM. While IBM didn't disclose how the data would be used, it is clear that there are integrations of weather data within many other aspects of the business (e.g., IoT) since weather data can affect device failure. Sometimes, even data that does not seem valuable can hide a wealth of information.

Keep these areas in mind as we explore how to build a good data strategy, as they will help guide your thinking.

Even the European Union has acknowledged the importance of data in the future, outlining their own data strategy. The goal is to create a single data marketplace to level the playing field in competing against the big tech companies that own vast amounts of valuable data ("European Data Strategy" n.d.).

Now that you are convinced that every business is a data business, it becomes clearer that a company needs an effective strategy to extract as much value as possible from the data it collects. Oftentimes, especially at the earliest stages of a business, data collection can be expensive in terms of time and money. A well-thought-out data strategy helps to zoom in on which data will unlock the most value and hopefully kick off the data flywheel.

Throughout my work, I have often seen these two types of situations, as shown in Table 3.1.

So, what do these two cases have in common? In both cases, a data strategy can save the day. In the first case, a data strategy would have

Table 3.1 Data strategy situations

	Situation 1	Situation 2
Use Case	A company wants to conduct a statistical analysis. As the problem is investigated, it becomes clear that data could have been collected to improve the analysis, but it is not available.	A start-up requires some sort of data science service. As the discussion about the system progresses, it becomes clear that the requested service depends on many different kinds of data. The collection and storage of this data expose new avenues for monetization that can help improve the start-up's revenue strategy.
Explanation	This is an example of what I like to call *data debt*, where the lack of planning for future projects has led to the company not collecting all of the necessary data. As we will see in the following, a good data strategy will describe the projects a company wishes to aim for in the coming 12–24 months, along with the data required to deliver good results on those projects. *Having a data scientist as part of the planning process will help make sure that you are covering your bases on all the data you should be collecting for the project.*	In this particular situation, the impact of planning for a specific data science project is that more opportunities are discovered to leverage the data in the overall revenue strategy. Often, the brainstorming around a data strategy can go backward and forward. While thinking of the data required for one project, you may discover other projects and opportunities open up using that same data.
Example	A car rental company wants to forecast demand for the upcoming months to create customized deals for each client. The company is not keeping information regarding the marital status and the age of its users. This information could have been very easily collected on its platform throughout all these years of operation. However, since this was not done, the company has to settle for a suboptimal model with reduced performance.	A common case is a recommender system. A recommender system can benefit from all kinds of information about the users: age, gender, purchases, and possibly other things. Designing the platform to improve information collected from its users results in an extensive and comprehensive database that can boost the recommender system's effectiveness and can also be used for other purposes. For example, this information could be used to better manage discount deals, improve advertising, or even enhance the user experience.

provided the company with tons of additional revenue. In the second case, a correctly implemented data strategy could provide the start-up with a competitive advantage in addition to increased revenues.

However, a data science strategy is less effective if it is not implemented from the early stages. This is why it is important to consider it as an integral plan of the product roadmap and the business plan. One of my favorite sayings is "failing to plan is planning to fail," which couldn't be more true for a data strategy.

How to Define a Data Strategy

Now that we've introduced the importance of having a data strategy, you must be wondering what the best process is to build a data strategy. There are many approaches that people favor online, each with its own pros and cons. The approach described as follows is one that we've had success with when working with small- to medium-sized businesses looking to build a roadmap for working with data.

Start With Your Business Strategy

A data strategy cannot exist in isolation of a coherent business strategy. The type of work you undertake will largely depend on objectives your business is looking to meet in the short- to medium term.

For example, imagine Company A (a B2C company) has just launched—or is about to launch—its first product to market. Presumably, one of their strategic priorities for the following year might be to rapidly acquire users and ensure that retention and engagement are high. Given these priorities, the data team must focus on building the right foundation to collect and analyze the necessary data to make rapid iterations on the product if necessary. In this example, this would form a core part of the data strategy.

Note that the business strategy will change from time to time, and so it is important that the data strategy also adapts to meet any new objectives or priorities.

If you have a clear idea of your strategic priorities as a business, then feel free to skip to the section on data use cases. Otherwise, in the following section, we will describe an exercise that should help you focus on what is most important for the business right now.

Exercise 1: Defining Your Strategic Priorities

First, a company needs to identify why it exists—what we'll call its *vision*. This vision is the North Star for the company, and it should answer the question, "What will the world look like in 10 years with our company?" It should be bold, grand, and aspirational because, even if you never get there, it gives everyone in your company a sense of direction and purpose.

Following the vision statement, you should create your mission statement. This is a more short-term-focused description of **why** the organization does what it does, **what** it does, **who** it does it for, and **how** it does it. The mission statement should feel as if it's within your grasp and is something you are clearly working toward in the present.

Lastly, from the mission statement, one can derive their strategic priorities. The whole point of defining the vision and mission is that you should start seeing a path from the organization's current state to reach that North Star and this path is your strategy! All that's left is defining the strategy into concrete priorities.

When going through this exercise with business owners in the past, we like to break down the business into its parts and get a feeling for where the areas for improvement are. The components we use to define a business are:

- Product
- Growth Marketing/Sales
- Internal Operations (People and processes)
- Business Model/Finance

These components will vary slightly depending on the type of business you're building, so change those as you see fit.

Once we've defined these components, the next step is to brainstorm some areas of work or improvement for each component (using a whiteboard tool or similar). It should come as no surprise that the more people that are involved from different parts of the business, the better the perspective you'll gain on each component.

However, keep in mind that each additional person will make the brainstorming session longer, making it more difficult to dive deeper into each employee's opinions.

The output of this brainstorming exercise will be a set of ideas and suggestions for areas of work for the business going forward. You should begin to see certain themes emerging within each of the components or even across components. Take some time with the group to cluster all the thoughts and ideas into logical groups and decide which ones likely deserve the most attention in the coming year. These should form the foundation of your business strategy.

Build Your Data Use Cases

From your strategic priorities, you can start to ideate what the data use cases could be to support the delivery of that strategy. A **data use case** is a well-contained and well-defined project that relates to completing one of your strategic objectives. The data use cases that you define will form your key priorities for the year ahead, and from these data use cases, you can begin to formulate a plan of your data activities.

Some examples of data use cases are:

- Build a self-serve analytics capability in the company;
- Reduce the cost of delivery of service for a particular product;
- Deliver a more personalized customer experience;
- Reduce customer churn.

A good number of data use cases would be 3 to 5 for a year, including 1 to 2 quick wins. A quick win data use case serves several purposes, namely that you can demonstrate near-immediate value from the data side of the business to get more buy-in from the rest of the business. Also, delivering a project end-to-end can help to uncover any unexpected issues before beginning work on any bigger projects.

Once you have identified your data use cases, you can start to break down what will be required to deliver each of them and what considerations to make before embarking on any of them. The areas you need to think about for each data use case are:

- Data requirements: Do you require any specific data to deliver the project? A data scientist will be able to guide you regarding the type of data that may be required for a project and the quantity.
- Key project resources: Think about the roles that will be required to deliver on your project—this could cover not only data engineers, data scientists, and data analysts but also any business owners, project/product managers, and so on. Also, think about which people in the business may be impacted by this project and need to be involved as stakeholders.
- Technology: Are there any technical dependencies before the project can be successfully implemented? Will the data architecture/infrastructure have to be modified to get all the required data?

It is useful to think of these areas for all data use cases together, so you can spot overlapping requirements across projects and better coordinate resources.

Data Architecture

Having a clear idea of how your data is architected is imperative for long-term success and continuous innovation. As your organization scales, the amount of data in your organization will scale, and often in a nonlinear manner since each new user could potentially be creating more data than previous users as your product grows and improves.

In the early stages of a company, the cost of switching from one database or architecture type to another is manageable. It can often be done without too much service downtime. Compare that with an organization like Slack, which spent three years (from 2017 to 2020) migrating their data architecture from active–active clusters to a tool called Vitess (Ganguli, Iaquinti, Zhou, and Chacon 2020). Clearly, the amount of due diligence, thought, and work put into this migration is eons above one that a start-up with fewer than a thousand users would have to make to move from NoSQL to a SQL database, for example.

The lesson here is that putting some careful consideration into your data and systems architecture early on can pay great dividends in the future. There are countless stories of organizations spending millions of dollars trying to fix data silos and merging data from countless sources to get a single version of the truth. Not to mention the potential sum in lost opportunities because of how difficult it was to quickly prototype and test new ideas.

The business case for putting some serious thought into the data architecture is irrefutable. However, in reality, there is a fine balancing act between spending endless hours designing the perfect architecture and implementing your best idea at the moment to move quickly.

If one follows the thinking of agile methodology, one can only make decisions under existing knowledge, and any assumption about what the future holds is just that, an assumption. Therefore, don't obsess over the perfect architecture, especially if there is still a lack of clarity around the product's future. Instead, it's more important to move quickly, test your assumptions, and keep iterating toward product-market fit.

Data Governance

Managing data across the organization is more than a technical or infrastructure challenge. It also relies heavily on the kind of *governance* a company puts in place to ensure that data is traceable, clearly defined, and accessible to only the people who need it. As with data architecture discussed previously, the scale of a data governance program should be proportional to the scale of data a business holds, meaning don't weigh down the business with too much process early on.

A good place to start on data governance early is building a companywide data dictionary. A data dictionary is a living document where all the raw and derived data that exists in an organization should be defined clearly. For any derived data, there should be an explanation of the original source of the data and any transformations applied to it. Building a data dictionary should highlight any areas of confusion or misunderstanding about the data and serve to align everyone in the company on where to search for data to create reports or metrics. It is also recommended to assign someone responsible for each data source. Those people can be contacted if any issues arise with the data or if people have questions or concerns.

Another crucial aspect of data governance is the processes required by law under regulations such as the General Data Protection Regulation (GDPR) or the California Consumer Privacy Act (CCPA). Again, a data dictionary will help massively in identifying what kind of personal data you hold about users and you can record the answers to questions such as:

- Why is this personal data necessary?
- How long is this data archived for after a user becomes inactive?
- What third-party software are we sharing this data with?

Managing an AI Project

The field of product management for software has been rising in popularity throughout the 20th and 21st centuries, as academics and entrepreneurs have been designing new approaches to manage the complexity of software projects. Most notably, this has led to the explosion of agile methodology, making it the go-to methodology for delivering products that users love.

While software development has had decades to learn and mature, AI product development is still in its infancy. As a result, AI product development presents new challenges not seen in software development: there are more unknowns, outcomes are nondeterministic, and there has been an influx of new tools, infrastructure, and processes to support AI development that people have to become familiar with.

However, perhaps most impactful is that AI shifts the concept of engineering from a deterministic process to a probabilistic one. With all these challenges in mind, one would think that the process to approach AI projects would need to differ from software. However, the reality is that most companies we've interacted with that are working on AI projects tend to shoehorn typical agile software methodology to fit with these new kinds of projects.

In this section, we will explore in further detail why AI projects differ from software projects, and how product management practices should shift to deal with this shifting paradigm.

Why Are AI Projects Different to Software Projects?

As mentioned previously, the difference can be described at a high level by the fact that AI development is much more of a probabilistic process than a deterministic one. The following four areas describe in more detail how these projects differ and will help to clarify this concept some more:

Unpredictability.   In traditional software projects, one can think of an overall project simplistically as a composition of functions where each function takes an input, applies some heuristics and processing to that input. As a result, the function returns an output.

When all these small unit functions are put together, one can create all sorts of wonderful applications. Since each function has been coded explicitly, it is simple enough to understand the behavior of each function by looking at what each line of code is doing. Doing so can help you understand not just typical test cases but also any edge cases that might cause the function to break. For example, if a function applies the logarithmic function to a set of inputs, any negative input will break it, so one can write some logic to reject any negative inputs.

If we continue this analogy in trying to explain the world of AI, one can think of AI as an approach to solving problems where we have pairs of input and output examples, and we're training a model to **replicate the function that converts the inputs into the outputs**. A simple case would be, if we had the pairs (1, 1), (2, 4), (3, 9), (7, 49), and (8, 64), then we would want our model to learn that the function is $y = x^2$.

In reality, the examples of input, output pairs that we work with represent much more complicated functions than this, which makes ML such a valuable tool in the toolkit. Now, say we've built a model, and we wanted to understand the behavior of the resulting function like was explained in the software project. We can no longer examine each line of code to understand what the function is doing since the model built is represented by some learned parameters that mix with the input in some mathematical formula.

This makes it much harder to understand the failure points of the function or model because it is more unclear how a model would behave with unseen inputs. This is particularly difficult with the recent rise in deep learning, as deep learning models are much more of a black-box approach than more simple ML approaches. Since the inner workings of the functions are hard to analyze and understand, it becomes much harder to understand and verify edge cases, as well as understand in what cases the model is likely to fail.

Another consequence of models learning the functions from input and output pairs is that ML models are never 100 percent correct (although they can come pretty close in some types of tasks). This means that organizations need to understand how to manage cases where models predict outputs incorrectly. In some cases, such as recommending new songs, the cost of a bad recommendation is not so high. However, in more serious applications, such as the automatic detection of cancer, a wrong prediction can have drastic consequences, so processes need to be put in place to deal with this.

Deterioration of Models.   ML models are called "models" because they are ultimately trying to accurately represent some behavior occurring in the real world. For example, a model that aims to forecast how many ice creams can be sold in a day will be modeling the behavior of ice cream demand across a population. Say that the temperature on a given day was given as an input to model the impact temperature has on ice cream sales. The model will likely find a positive correlation between temperature and ice cream sales, and sales will, in all likelihood, be predicted relatively accurately.

We all know that the world we live in is incredibly complex and that behaviors change over time. This means that any model trained on historical data will be more and more out of date as the world changes and adapts to new circumstances. In the case of our ice cream model, there could be an increased awareness over time that ice creams are unhealthy because of their sugar content, leading to a slight decrease in ice cream sales over time. Our model would not accurately represent the real world since a day with the same temperature as a day a year ago will lead to fewer sales. This means our model will need to be **retrained** to capture the change in behavior.

This phenomenon is extremely common across all areas of ML and leads to models needing to be retrained periodically for the accuracy to not deteriorate over time. A more representative example of this in the real world is the example of fraud detection, where criminals are always coming up with new ways to defraud institutions; hence models need to adapt to be able to detect these new types of fraud. This reality means that a model is never in its "final state," adding another layer of complexity to AI projects.

Hard to Forecast.   It may be tempting to think that because one solution to an AI problem worked to solve another problem very similar to your own, this solution will also work on your problem. For example, you may be building an e-commerce store and find an implementation of a recommender system built on another store that has worked well. However, the reality is that the underlying distribution of the data used to train these models is different. Therefore, you will need a different solution for your specific problem.

Consider this example further. On the surface, the data needed to train the recommender system is almost identical. There is a group of products with some product metadata. Next, there are the users, each with their own characteristics. Lastly, there's a set of interactions between users and the products. Even so, the same implementation of a recommender system works for one website but not for another. How can this be?

There could be many explanations for this phenomenon, but ultimately it comes down to the fact that the distributions generating this data are not the same. In layman's terms, people on one website could be completely different from those on the other website, with various purchasing behaviors and motivations. One model might be great at accurately representing the population's behavior on one website but be bad for the other website. Sometimes you may get lucky, and a slightly different set of the model hyperparameters could be enough to solve your specific problem. Other times, you might need to look for an entirely different algorithm to solve your problem.

Hard to Measure Progress.   Even as an experienced data scientist, it can sometimes be very hard to fully understand why a model isn't performing well. Typically a fair amount of manual inspection is required to figure out why some training examples are being predicted inaccurately, which could even mean looking example by example at what features may be confusing the model. This reality means that it is even harder to determine what changes will lead to any significant improvements in performance.

It is possible to struggle for weeks as you run several experiments and tune certain model parameters that result in only a 1 to 2 percent improvement in the model. Until you suddenly discover a new input feature that improves the model by 10 to 20 percent! Progress in an AI project is very chronologically nonlinear, and it can be challenging at the beginning of a project to know when you'll make that breakthrough that will make your model viable to deploy.

I have witnessed many projects where, for weeks, it felt like that breakthrough was coming, to no avail. When is it the time to decide that enough effort has been expended on one solution hypothesis? There are many possible rabbit holes to go down for any solution, making this question very difficult to answer. The "definition of done" is certainly not clear for an ML project, as your team may feel that the extra performance can be obtained. But at what cost? It is imperative to come back to business value to determine whether pursuing that extra model performance will deliver any benefit.

Principles for Agile AI Development.   While the previous section describes the difficulties of estimating and delivering an AI project relative to a software project, there are some tactics that organizations can implement to give themselves a leg up when it comes to becoming an AI-powered organization (Table 3.2).

Data Science Processes.   There are many different ways to implement a data science project. This has led to the creation of some processes that formalize some of the steps required. In this section, we will explore some of these processes.

Table 3.2 Agile AI development

Define your company's mission and near-term strategy	This topic was covered extensively in the first section of the chapter, but it is so important that it should be included here again. Not only should you take the time to define this, but once you have it, make sure that the ML applications that you work on directly impact your north star metrics.
Follow the data science hierarchy of needs	The data science hierarchy of needs (Rogati 2017) places AI at the top of the pyramid (think self-actualization if you are familiar with Maslow's hierarchy of needs). Before you can effectively build AI into your organization, crucial aspects need to be developed, such as data collection mechanisms and the ability to run data analytics on your connected data. Figure 3.1 shows the full data science hierarchy of needs that you should follow as a path toward building an AI-driven organization.
Build data labeling into your product	Building labeled data sets for ML applications is expensive, particularly when you must outsource the labeling to external services. If you can build a mechanism in your product that encourages users to label data (e.g., categorizing a transaction in your banking app), you will organically build a large enough dataset to train an ML model.
Make your first AI project a simple one	Andrew Ng, the cofounder of Coursera and Landing.ai, preaches this tactic in his playbook to usher organizations into the world of AI. There are many direct and indirect benefits of working on a simple AI project first, but mainly it (a) delivers immediate value to the organization, (b) secures buy-in from stakeholders that AI is a valuable area to invest in, and (c) delivers a successful project will boost team morale and have knock-on effects for future projects.
Make sure the problem is very well defined	The more precisely you can describe the problem you're trying to solve, the more you can narrow down approaches that may solve the problem. Consider what edge cases your algorithm might face and how it should approach those. It really helps to try to solve the problem manually first, as a team, so you have a few examples to base your discussion on and start to exclude or include potential solution approaches.
Do the simplest thing that could possibly work	When starting any project (this also applies to non-AI or ML projects), it often helps to refer back to the 80/20 rule and think about the simplest thing that gets you most of the way there with little development. This tactic has two clear advantages: 1. You may find that the simplest method you can think of already delivers enough value. Otherwise, you have a better idea of how far from the target performance this simple method gets you, which can be useful to understand the complexity of the problem. 2. A simple method will force you to think more about the whole end-to-end solution (data inputs/outputs, pipelines) rather than focus on building a complicated algorithm. This will uncover any unexpected surprises that might arise when deploying this algorithm, and these can be handled in parallel while the algorithm is improved and research is underway.

The data science
HIERARCHY OF NEEDS

AI,
deep
learning

A/B testing,
experimentation
simple ML algorithms

Learn/optimize

Analytics, metrics,
segments, aggregates,
features, training data

Aggregate/label

Explore/transform   Cleaning, anomaly detection, prep

Reliable data flow, infrastructure,
pipelines, ETL, structure, and
unstructured data storage

Move/store

Instrumentation, logging, sensors,
external data, user-generated content

Collect

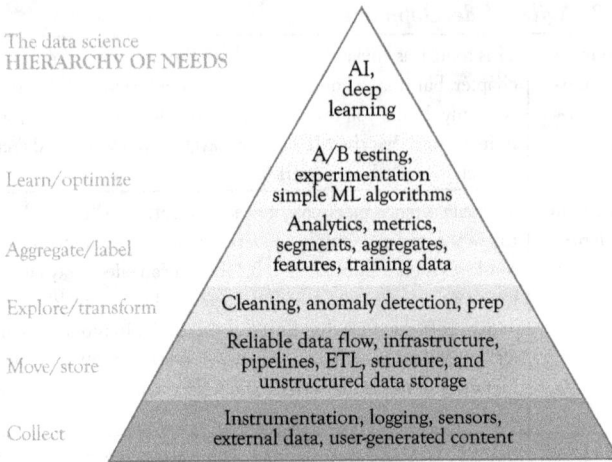

Figure 3.1 Data science hierarchy of needs

The processes outlined here are all slight variations on each other while following a common set of principles on how to approach data science projects. If you are to take anything from this section, it should be these principles. The final processes should fit your project style and requirements rather than shifting your ways of working to fit these processes. These processes are guidelines and best practices, but real projects are messy so always think about what types of processes will suit your specific set of circumstances.

Process 1: CRISP-DM.   CRISP-DM (Cross-Industry Standard Process for Data Mining) is perhaps the most popular process used to plan a typical data science project. The purpose of CRISP-DM is to clearly define the phases that make up a data science project and to understand how those phases interact with each other.

Unlike the Microsoft Team Data Science Process described as follows, CRISP-DM does not concern itself with the lower-level details of how work is managed or the roles and responsibilities in the team. Instead, CRISP-DM is a high-level framework that will help you to understand what kind of work is carried out in each phase of the project and also the deliverables that could be expected. Above all, though, CRISP-DM emphasizes the iterative nature of a data science project and is flexible to move between phases in response to new learnings and findings during the project.

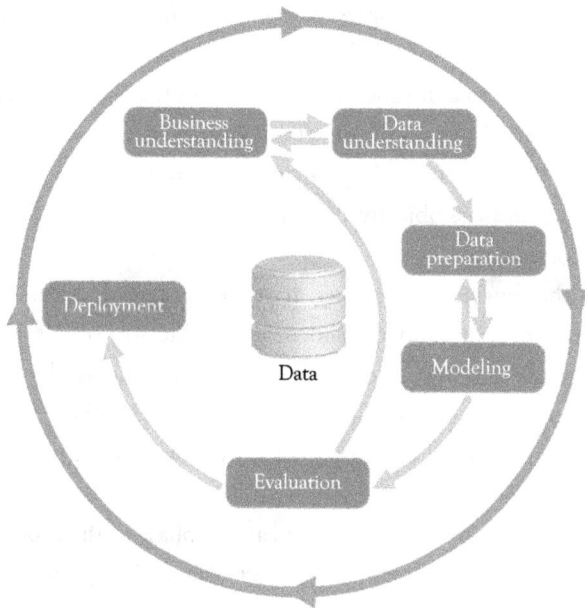

Figure 3.2 Six main phases of the CRISP-DM process

Six main phases are described as part of the CRISP-DM process (Figure 3.2):

1. Business Understanding
2. Data Understanding
3. Data Preparation
4. Modeling
5. Evaluation
6. Deployment

Business Understanding: The first phase sets out the context for the project by focusing on three main areas: (a) defining the business objectives, (b) identifying the project requirements, and (c) building a project plan.

Setting clear business objectives is arguably the most important part of the process, because these will be continually referred back to throughout the project to make important decisions. Think about a primary goal that you are seeking to achieve and any related questions that would be useful to address. Once you have these, consider which metrics will most accurately track the progress toward achieving the primary business objective. It is dangerous to define a project outcome that is not measurable as it may lead to a misunderstanding within the team of whether the project is moving in the right direction. Also, it is common for project teams to go down rabbit holes that may not contribute to moving the needle on the business objective, so having metrics to track will be useful to course correct.

Once the business objectives have been agreed upon, consider the key requirements and dependencies for the project. It is best to have a data scientist involved in this process to validate the feasibility of the project with the specified data and resources. The requirements can be split into several categories, such as project resources, data, and computing resources.

While there are many uncertainties at this phase of the project, it can be helpful to draw up a high-level project plan with key milestones you want to hit. As data science projects are quite exploratory and uncertain in nature, make sure to be realistic in your timelines and add a good amount of buffer to avoid unexpected delays.

Data Understanding: This is always the first step of any data scientist when approaching a new problem. The outcome of this phase is to verify that there is enough data and that it is of a high enough quality to build accurate models.

Common pitfalls in the data are variables having lots of missing values, the correct variables not being collected for the project, or there being noise in the data due to some error in the collection process. The data understanding phase should seek to extract these insights and validate any preconceived assumptions about what the data is describing. A typical output of this phase is a report that highlights the findings and any immediate actions that might need to be taken to correct errors in the data.

Data Preparation: The precursor to the modeling phase is the preparation phase. A data scientist will select the appropriate data from the various identified data sources and perform data cleaning and wrangling exercises to transform it into a state that will allow it to be inputted into a data science model.

This phase will be repeated several times throughout the project, as you will undoubtedly learn and experiment with different data points and different processing methods to improve modeling results. You will often hear the phrase "Garbage In, Garbage Out," and this is also true of modeling—often, the best improvements in data science models are generated by carefully selecting the input data and processing it in creative ways rather than fine-tuning the model parameters.

Modeling: The modeling phase involves researching and developing the most appropriate models for the use case. There is a lot of uncertainty in this phase of the project, as models don't always transfer across use cases, even when the use cases are very similar. Owing to this, it is important to start with simple models and then iterate from there as you build up an understanding of the limitations of the simple models. There are many open-source libraries and packages that make it easy to get started with prebuilt models; we have listed a few at the end of the document relating to each use case.

Before beginning any model development, make sure you have a clear understanding of which model evaluation metrics will be used to compare and select the best models, for example do you prioritize precision or recall? This depends vastly on your use case and the cost of different errors.

As described previously, the modeling phase and data preparation phase are tightly linked. Each model is based on slightly different assumptions of the data, so the data may need to be processed differently for each model. Furthermore, models can be improved through better feature engineering (which variables you feed into the model from the raw input data).

Evaluation: As opposed to the model evaluation that forms a part of the modeling phase, the evaluation phase here is about determining how well the project is measuring up to the overall business objectives set out at the beginning of the project. At this stage, you will undoubtedly have learned a lot about the data, and the complexities of the project, meaning you may choose to revisit the business objectives slightly based on your learnings.

Perhaps in this stage, it would make sense to test the model in a real, lightweight setting with real users. While the model may be performing well in a development environment, it may not perform as well as you expect in a production environment if the data doesn't quite match real life or there are any factors that have been overlooked while developing the model.

Deployment: If you get to the stage you are happy with the model results, congratulations! You are almost at the point where you can derive business value from the project. The final stage of the project is the deployment stage, where you must decide how the model will be running in production. Common questions to ask here are:

- How often will the model be run on new data? Batch predictions or real time?
- How will the model communicate with the input and output systems? Does an API (Application Programming Interface) need to be designed?
- How will you monitor the performance of the model over time? Who will be responsible for this?
- How often does the model need to be retrained? Ideally, this question should be answered during the evaluation phase as you understand how the model performance decays over time.

Process 2: Microsoft Team Data Science Process.   Microsoft defines the Team Data Science Process (Microsoft n.d.) as follows:

The Team Data Science Process (TDSP) is an agile, iterative data science methodology to deliver predictive analytics solutions and intelligent applications efficiently. TDSP helps improve team collaboration and learning by suggesting how team roles work best together. TDSP includes best practices and structures from Microsoft and other industry leaders to help toward the successful implementation of data science initiatives. The goal is to help companies fully realize the benefits of their analytics program.

The process is defined by the following key components:

1. A data science life cycle definition.
2. A standardized project structure.
3. Infrastructure and resources for data science projects.
4. Tools and utilities for project execution.

For the context of what we've been discussing in this chapter, the data science life cycle definition is the most relevant. Components 2 to 4 are incredibly useful when getting to the implementation, and I encourage you to check it out on Microsoft's website. For the rest of this section, we'll only focus on the life cycle.

The life cycle defined in this project borrows a lot from the CRISP-DM methodology described in the last section but reinforces the importance of making the process *iterative* and, above all, iterating between each main phase of the project rather than only iterating through the full cycle. The life cycle can be summarized by the following diagram (Figure 3.3).

As you can see from the diagram, the four main phases of the life cycle are:

- Business Understanding
- Data Acquisition and Understanding
- Modeling
- Deployment

This can be mapped almost like-for-like to CRISP-DM, with the only exceptions being that Data Understanding and Data Preparation have

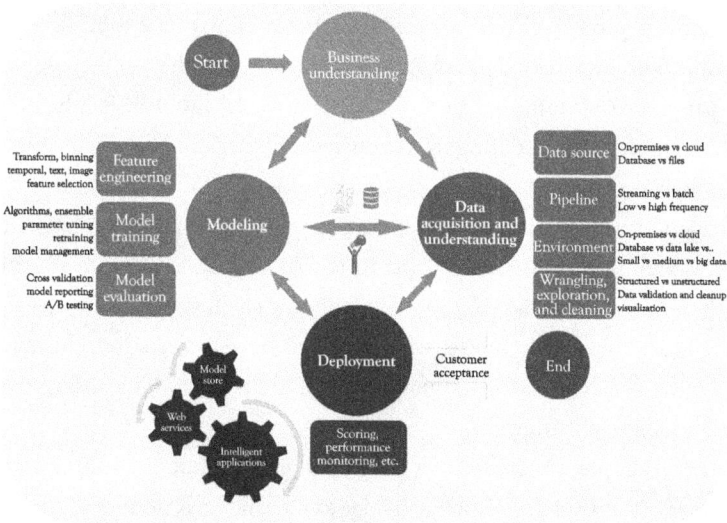

Figure 3.3 Data science life cycle

been collapsed into Data Acquisition and Understanding, and Modeling and Evaluation have been collapsed into Modeling. Given this similarity, please refer to the previous section for detailed explanations on the kind of activities carried out in each phase.

The important area to emphasize in this section is the iterative nature of the process. Being agile in the way you approach data science development will undoubtedly give you an advantage in delivering quality projects on time. It is very rare to go through the process once. It would mean having the perfect problem definition, knowing exactly what data you need to solve the problem, and then developing and deploying the perfect model. That doesn't happen. There will be surprises and lessons along the way that will change previously held assumptions in the process.

In the Business Understanding phase, you will come up with an initial plan for how you're going to solve the problem that you've set out and what data you will need to train a model. Once the plan is created, the first step is to explore the data you have identified to see if the quality and quantity are sufficient. The findings from this phase will provide some new information, such as whether there is any missing data for the data points you wish to extract or whether there is an imbalance of training examples (e.g., the majority of your users are male; therefore, your algorithm might suffer in accuracy for female users). It is vital to revisit the documents prepared in the Business Understanding phase to update the assumptions and the proposed approaches. Likewise, the modeling phase might prove that some method of approaching the problem is infeasible, which would need updating in the Business Understanding documents.

However, the most common feedback loop from the diagram is the interaction between the Data Acquisition and Understanding phase and the Modeling phase. As explained in the AI Principles section, starting with the simplest model you can think of on a small subset of your entire data is beneficial. The model will likely not be very accurate. However, exploring the model's errors may give you a clue as to what other data points will help it improve.

For example, I worked on a project where we were building recommender systems to recommend books to children. We found, from initial models, that the recommendations were irrelevant for children since their preferences change so quickly as they grow up. From this, we were able to identify that knowing the child's age would improve the model considerably by making more age-specific recommendations.

Over the lifetime of a project, there will be many iterations across this loop, and you want to make sure that you record the findings along the way so that you have some traceability of the data points that have been tested and what approaches have worked or not worked.

Lastly, once you have a satisfactory model and are ready to deploy, there will be some back and forth between the Deployment phase and the Modeling and Data Acquisition and Understanding phases as you try to discover the optimal approach to deploying a model. The model will need to access new data from your production databases, so you need to consider how and where the data is stored and where the predictions of the model will be stored. Similarly, will the model be deployed through an API or run as a scheduled job to train and output new predictions? The response to this may require some changes in the Modeling phase to ensure the model is suitable for your requirements.

Microsoft has released a Github repository that anyone can use to get started with the process: https://github.com/Azure/Azure-TDSP-ProjectTemplate.

Process 3: Tesseract Academy's 2-Actor Process.   Tesseract Academy's 2-actor process focuses not so much on how the data strategy interacts with the business but more on the interpersonal dynamics between the data scientist and the business leader.

The previous processes do a good job of breaking down the steps required to complete a data science project. Tesseract Academy's process takes a more person-centric view, focusing a lot on the challenges and misinterpretations that can take place between the two main actors of any data science project: the key business stakeholder and the data science lead.

This process is an excellent complement to the other processes outlined here and can help you uncover any challenges that might arise. The process assumes that a company does not have a data science function and can be very useful for organizations embarking on that journey. Companies that have been working with data for a long time will find that many of the challenges outlined in this process might not exist for them.

In this process, there are two main actors and four steps. The main actors are the **domain expert** (or key business stakeholder) and the **data scientist** (or, in the case of a data science team, the team leader).

The four steps are outlined as follows. Under each step, you will find the person who is responsible for completing it.

1. Problem definition
   a. Domain expert
2. Choosing the right data (data management)
   a. Domain expert
   b. Data scientist
3. Solution of the problem
   a. Data scientist
4. Creating value through actionable insights
   a. Data scientist AND domain expert

Problem definition: This is where the key problem is defined. This is done by the domain expert (and key business stakeholder). Why is it the domain expert instead of the data scientist? Because no one can speak better about the problems of the business than someone who is actually part of the business. While a data scientist might bring some external knowledge, the domain expert is the one who should really understand all the intricacies of their organization. This means that they should be able to pose a list of relevant problems/challenges.

The data scientist may have worked in this field before and might have some great ideas, which can be used straight out of the box. However, even if that's the case, the domain expert needs to have at least a clear idea of the business problems to really own the proposed solution and prioritize any suggestions accordingly.

There is no requirement here to be 100 percent specific. For example, a domain expert who lacks an understanding of data science might find it challenging to provide an unambiguous description of the business's problems. That's fine, as long as they can give an accurate picture of the overall business and some key performance indicators.

The danger here is being vague and unable to explain what the expected key metrics or results are to the data scientist. Solving the challenge requires the data scientist to make sure they are optimizing for the right target and then communicating these results to the domain expert so that the benefit becomes clear. This first step is crucial in achieving this goal.

Choosing the right data (data management): This is tricky because it requires the synergy of both the data scientist and the domain expert. In an ideal world, the business has followed a data strategy from day zero. The data is clean and of good quality. The domain is relatively simple, and there is no noise in the data. Unfortunately, this is the exception rather than the rule.

In most cases, a business will not have followed a data strategy. This means that the data scientist might encounter many issues, such as:

1. Missing values;
2. Important and useful variables not being collected;
3. Data being collected at the wrong level of granularity (e.g., month instead of day).

Similarly, there is a significant danger here coming from the domain. One of the authors worked with a company producing a radar device. He developed an algorithm for them, but when the company changed the chipset, the algorithm stopped working. The problem was due to the noise inherent in the two chipsets and some other version differences in the hardware. Both the author and the company were unaware that upgrading the chipset wouldn't improve the algorithm, but rather it would require complete retraining.

So, the best way to walk through this step is through a back-and-forth between the data scientist and the domain expert. Make no assumptions! Do not assume that the data is correct, accurate, or lacks noise. Be very skeptical of any early, very successful results. It is more likely that you have data leakage rather than amazing data.

An example of data leakage is when an input variable correlates very highly with the outcome variable but wouldn't usually be available at the test time. For example, if you are forecasting quarterly sales and someone is adding a binary variable indicating whether sales were high or low, this would cause performance to spike. But this variable was created after looking into the past.

Solution of the problem: This step comes down to the data scientist. If the previous steps have been done correctly, the following things will be in place:

1. A clear definition of the problem and the business.
2. A good, clean set of data.

The data scientist now needs to do the following:

1. Identify the key metrics of success.
2. Solve the problem using a variety of data science methods.

This takes us to step 4.

Creating value through actionable insights: So far, the domain expert–data scientist duo have achieved the following:

1. Built a common understanding of the problem.
2. Checked the quality of the data.
3. Created a solution.

Now it's time for the two actors to work in complete synergy. The data scientist has to explain to the domain expert how the solution really addresses the problem outlined in step 1. The decision maker has to understand and approve this solution. The solution needs to be translated in measurable results. This way, the domain expert can integrate it into the overall company strategy, and the data scientist can have a measure of performance to use as a benchmark when further improving the solution.

Case Studies

Let's take a look at a few case studies to make all the above easier to understand.

Case Study 1: The Recommender System

A recommender system is an invaluable tool for any e-commerce business and beyond. Spotify uses a recommender system to best identify the songs you are going to like. Amazon is using a recommender system to recommend products to you. And Netflix uses a recommender system to try and predict what movies or shows you will watch for hours.

So, in this case study, we will deal with a fictional company called Zookla. Zookla is an online retailer of sports clothes and equipment. The company consists of 10 people and includes software developers, business development, and the CEO, who is still very much involved in day-to-day operations. The company recently raised $5 million and wants to establish a data science function. The first thing they care most about is creating a recommender system.

Zookla hires a data scientist to deal with this on a six-month contract.

Analysis: Tesseract Academy's 2-Actor Model

We will analyze the project from the perspective of Tesseract Academy's 2-actor model. Here is a reminder of the process:

1. Problem definition
   a. Domain expert
2. Choosing the right data (data management)
   a. Domain expert
   b. Data scientist
3. Solution of the problem
   a. Data scientist
4. Creating value through actionable insights
   a. Data scientist AND domain expert

So, let's see the good and the bad scenario for each step.

Problem Definition: Good Scenario

In a good scenario, the CEO has a good idea of what a recommender system is and how it could improve profits. The CEO also has a good idea of what this would look like on the screen. There are many ways to present a recommender system. For example, Amazon uses the following two ways: "frequently bought together" and "customers who bought this also bought," As depicted in Figure 3.4.

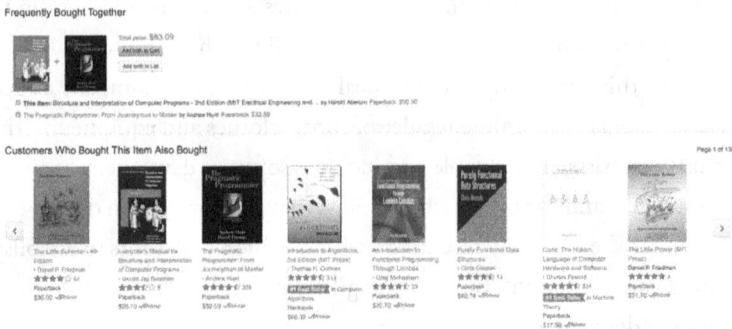

Figure 3.4 Example of the Amazon recommender system in action

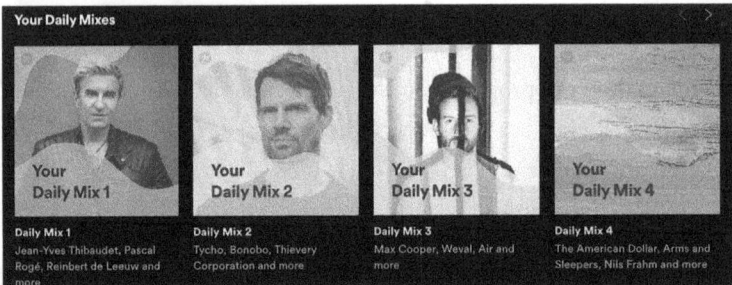

Figure 3.5 Examples of the Spotify recommender system in action

Spotify, on the other hand, creates custom playlists based on the songs you like, as shown in Figure 3.5.

And obviously, there are many other ways to present recommendations, such as a list or tiles (e.g., Netflix).

The way recommendations are presented interacts with the UI/UX (User Interface/User Experience). And the way the UX/UI is designed affects how the data is collected. It's essential to be aware of these interplays.

Also, finally, it helps if the CEO has good intuition or the company has done some preliminary research on useful patterns (e.g., customer segmentation). These can not only help inform the design of a recommender system, but they can also be used to create a simple rule-based recommender that could be used as a benchmark for a more advanced version.

Problem Definition: Bad Scenario

In the bad scenario, the CEO falls into one of these two groups:

1. They say they "want to do something useful with data," but they are not sure what that is.
2. They say they want a recommender system, but they are oblivious to all the details and issues that this entails.

The first scenario is pretty common and most data scientists would be prepared for it. In this case, the data scientist will take some time to explain data science to the CEO, learn more about the business, and discover the best way forward. The CEO would have been better off if they had done this preparatory work before hiring a data scientist because the result is one to two months of work.

The second case is much trickier. The CEO might be confident in what they want, but they might be ignoring a lot of critical topics:

1. They might be ignoring the interaction between the recommender system and UX/UI in how results are displayed and how data are collected.
2. They have no real understanding of their customers.
3. They are not sure what metrics they are after. What would success look like for this project?

So, the first point can be a huge problem if, for example, the website requires an extensive redesign to display recommendations and collect relevant data. Points 2 and 3 often come together. Sometimes, there is lots of enthusiasm about a project, but the client does not really know what they're looking for. Is it simply more sales? More engagement? How much more?

It is not possible to forecast the level of success. However, it is not uncommon for a project to finish and for the client to realize they are not happy with the results because they couldn't verbalize their expectations from the onset. For example, if a client believes that a recommender system would double sales, this is likely unrealistic. The data scientist could explain what might be more feasible or how they could create a constantly improving system.

There are cases where clients hold latent beliefs about the expectations surrounding new AI systems, but even they are not aware of them until the last minute when things don't seem to be going the way they wanted them to go.

Case Study 2: Forecasting Demand

Forecasting demand is a common problem in industries like retail. If a business can successfully do it, it can optimize its supply chains and orders to maximize margins. Let's take the example of Leotard Clothes. This is a retailer that sells cat-inspired clothes.

They have limited space in their warehouses, and producing clothes takes a significant amount of time and resources due to the special fabrics used. Also, they use many outside contractors, which means that costs will vary according to manufacturing volume. Manufacturing more clothes than the demand will significantly increase monthly costs, but if they manufacture fewer clothes, the company can still make a profit. Another issue with contractors is that there were shortages of material in some cases. Leotard Clothes would ideally like to preorder fabric a few months in advance.

Hence for them, predicting demand is vital so that they know how many clothes to manufacture each month.

Let's see how Leotard Clothes can use the CRISP-DM approach to forecast demand.

Analysis: CRISP-DM

Let's revisit the CRISP-DM process. Six main phases are described as part of the CRISP-DM process (Figure 3.6):

1. Business Understanding
2. Data Understanding

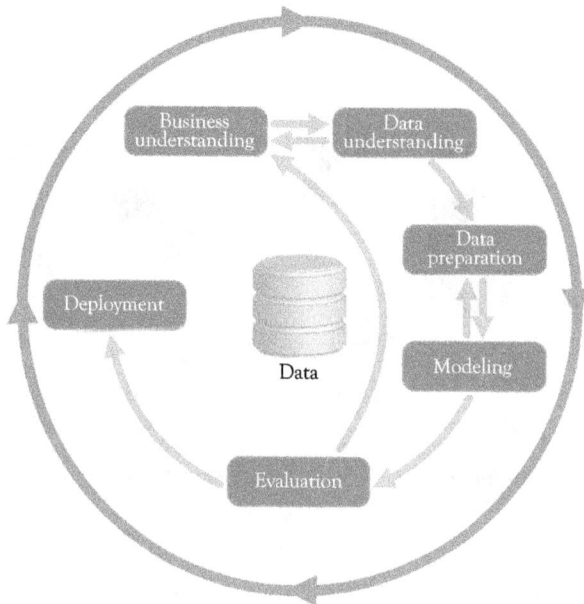

Figure 3.6 Six main phases of the CRISP-DM process

3. Data Preparation
4. Modeling
5. Evaluation
6. Deployment

The first step (business understanding) is key. While forecasting is what the company wants to do, it wants to do this within the context of its operations. This means that forecasting demand is being used to optimize the allocation of resources.

This step is directly connected to the fifth step (evaluation). Why is that? Because when evaluating a ML pipeline, we need to identify how results are translated into business actions. Since forecasting is a regression problem, the reported metrics will be something like the Mean Absolute Error or the Root Mean Squared Error. But what is a good score? This is very much business related.

There are domains where a difference of 1 percent in performance can translate into millions of dollars. In other fields, a difference of 5 percent

	Business understanding	Data ingest and understanding	Modeling	Deployment	Acceptance
Project lead	Create template repository	Provision data infrastructure			Checkpoint project · Transition to production support
Data scientist		Provision compute assets (DS VM) · Data ingest and explore · Data summary report	Feature engineering · Model dev · Model report	Deploy scoring process · Monitor health and metrics · Dashboard	Check in final artifacts · Decommission compute assets
Project manager	Create project charter · Project charter				Finalize documentation · Project final report
Solutions architect		Design solution architecture · Solution architecture diagram	Develop data pipeline	Deploy pipeline	

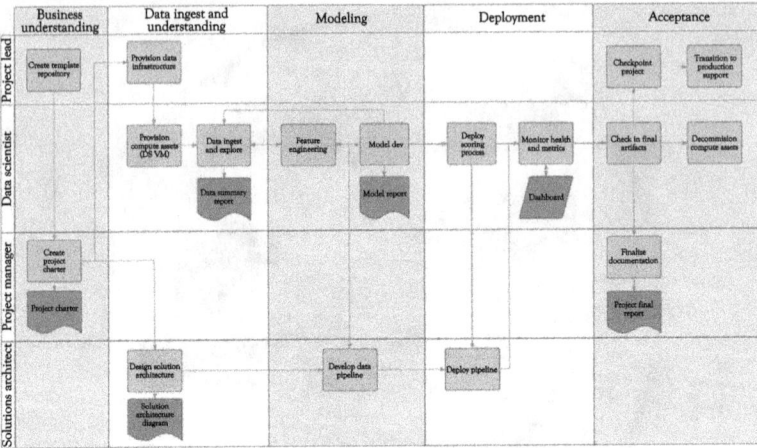

Figure 3.7 Example of the Teams Data Science Process

might not mean much. In this particular example, the interest is in ensuring the following:

1. There is enough space in the warehouse.
2. Point 1 requires that the clothes are sold, and there is enough demand.
3. Point 1 also requires that the materials ordered align with the demand.

Hence, while we are predicting demand, the key challenge is how to make sure that the warehouse has enough space. So, this should be our main focus.

The rest of the steps in CRISP-DM are pretty standard in any data science project. Most data scientists will follow a similar process, even if they do not explicitly phrase it. We leave the analysis here because the Teams Data Science Process (discussed in Figure 3.7) covers some of these steps in greater depth.

Case Study 3: Natural Language Processing

Let's see how we could use the Teams Data Science Process to break down a given problem. Suppose we are dealing with an online clothes retailer called Zappo. The company is interested in running natural language processing on its social media accounts to better understand how they could be improved.

The first thing we notice is that there are four actors:

1. Project lead
2. Data scientist
3. Project manager
4. Solution architect

According to the process, the solution architect is responsible for ensuring a proper business understanding within the company. The process also defines some technical tasks that need to be achieved. For example, in the first step, the repository is created by the project lead instead of the data scientist, hence clearly separating responsibilities between the different roles.

In our case, the project lead needs to define what would be measured. For example, the company could choose to measure:

1. Sentiment analysis on user comments about its products.
2. Prediction of post engagement.
3. Time series analysis of engagement metrics.

So, we can immediately see that a general task of "using NLP to study social media" immediately breaks down into multiple different tasks. Each task should be treated separately. So, we can assume that the company in this use case decided to focus on the first task and go with sentiment analysis.

The second stage of the process involves the data scientist, who is responsible for producing a report. You can see that the first output of the data scientist is something that can be easily communicated to the management. The process clearly places significant emphasis on business understanding. At the same time, the solution architect will start working on the deployment specifics. In our case, this would be about the choice of database, setting up APIs to extract data from social media, and so on.

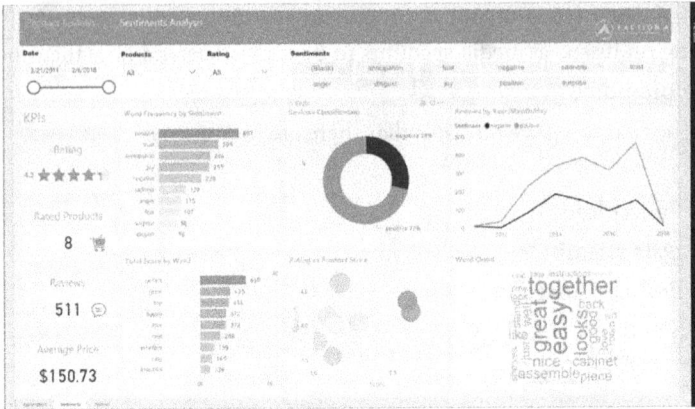

Figure 3.8 A sentiment analysis dashboard
Source: Faction A 2018

The third step, modeling, consists of the data scientist running various sentiment analyses algorithms and comparing them. The output of this stage is a model report. Again, this helps keep track of how the project is progressing and communicating value to the business stakeholders.

The fourth step is deployment. In the third and the fourth steps, the main actors are the data scientist and the solution architect. The results, in this case, are communicated through a dashboard. The dashboard in our example could contain things such as classifications of reviews and a word cloud (Figure 3.8).

In the final stage, acceptance, the project lead and the project manager come back into play and bring everything together. A final report, written by the project manager, ensures that everything has been documented and the project can be finalized.

Case Study 4: Computer Vision and Algorithmic Bias

This case study will investigate three interesting challenges: computer vision, algorithmic bias, and data privacy.

Let's say that you are developing a piece of software that can extract information about the people in a retail store by using cameras installed in the store. This application can be used to calculate not only footfall but also the characteristics of the different people in the store, such as gender, age, race, and so on.

You have decided that you will use a commoditized solution for computer vision such as Google Vision or IBM Watson.

Something important to note here is that this is a special case. The reason is that this use case also touches upon issues of compliance, regulation, and ethics. Let's see why:

First, the company will have to make sure that the individuals' private data is not stored. This refers to the actual images or inferences made about an individual, such as age. It is likely that, depending on the geographical region, the exact legal requirements will be different, but there will undoubtedly be various legal complications.

Secondly, the application should make sure that it is not biased against certain types of people. It is well known that computer vision algorithms can be biased against minorities. A famous article by *Time* demonstrated how a computer vision API might mistake Oprah Winfrey for a man, for example ("Artificial Intelligence Has a Problem With Gender and Racial Bias" n.d.).

Given that the main challenges here touch upon different parts of the business, Tesseract Academy's 2-actor model could be very useful. The benefit of this model is that it is very flexible, so it can also be applied in circumstances where the challenge is not only of a technical nature. The key point behind this process is that it lays out all the challenges that the project might face. Therefore, the decision maker and the data scientist can make sure they are on the same page when tackling a particular challenge.

Analysis: Tesseract Academy's 2-Actor Model

So, let's revisit the process.

1. Problem definition
   a. Domain expert
2. Choosing the right data
   a. Domain expert
   b. Data scientist
3. Solution of the problem
   a. Data scientist

4. Creating value through actionable insights
   a. Data scientist AND domain expert

Problem Definition.   In this particular case, the core problem definition is clear. The business owner wants to know specific statistics about the people in a store, such as gender, age, and race.

However, the core problem definition needs to be extended. We also need to add:

1. Data privacy
2. Elimination of bias

These points are going to inform the solution to the problem.

The decision maker has also defined that the business should go for a commoditized solution, instead of developing their own solution internally.

Choosing the Right Data.   In this case, the data is a direct feed coming from cameras located inside the store. Therefore, the cameras must be of high quality, and the network must have enough bandwidth to feed the data to the API.

Data privacy falls under this step. Remember that data management involves both the decision maker and the data scientist. While the data scientist is responsible for the technical aspects, the decision maker needs to ensure that the business is compliant.

What they both need to decide upon is how the data can be fed to the API and what are the implications of the different choices. Is the data going to be stored somewhere and then sent? Or is it going to be sent in real time? How does this affect costs for data storage and network usage?

Solution to the Problem.   Given the extended problem definition and the constraints imposed by the decision maker, the data scientist has to define the right solution and come up with an attack plan. In this case, the attack plan does not involve data analysis but rather the comparison of different solutions in the market.

More specifically, the data scientist will have to run A/B tests between all major computer vision service providers and identify which ones seem to work best. The data scientist might have to go to the store and test these systems in real time in realistic conditions.

Creating Value Through Actionable Insights. Typically, actionable insights are derived after data has been analyzed. In this case, the data scientist and the decision maker will have to constantly monitor the system or the first few months of operation to ensure it works as expected. All sorts of problems could arise that could affect the result, but that might not be related to the API, such as issues with the cameras.

The following Table 3.3 summarizes all of the above insights.

Table 3.3 Summary of Tesseract Academy's 2-actor model

Problem definition	1. Get statistics 2. Data privacy 3. No bias
Choosing the right data (data management)	1. Data feed from cameras 2. Data privacy
Solution of the problem	1. Discover the best API 2. Test APIs in realistic conditions
Creating value through actionable insights	1. Ensure that the API works as expected 2. Revisit the model if required

Key Takeaways

- Data strategy is defined as "*a **living** document that defines how the business is setting itself up, both from a technical and organizational perspective, to proactively manage and leverage data towards the long-term business strategy.*"
- Data science development is different to software development. Managing a data science project requires following a data science process.
- There are different processes for data science, some popular ones being CRISP-DM and the Tesseract Academy's 2-actor process.

CHAPTER 4

Hiring/Managing Data Scientists and Building a Data-Centric Culture

To be able to hire a good data scientist, you first need to understand what to look for. You need to know not only the traits of a good data scientist but also what skills they should have. Furthermore, to manage data scientists effectively, you need to understand what drives them. That's exactly what we'll be looking at in this chapter.

Understanding How a Data Scientist's Mind Works

A good data scientist needs to have quite a few skills, but some are more important than others. Data scientists need to have math and statistics knowledge, hacking skills, and substantive expertise. If even one of these is missing, then, while the person might be incredibly smart, they are still not a data scientist.

Hacking Skills

When we say hacking, we're not actually referring to someone having the ability to get through the Pentagon's firewalls. What we actually mean is that a data scientist needs to have outstanding computer knowledge.

However, this doesn't necessarily mean that they need a degree in computer science. After all, plenty of people are excellent hackers or have made a fortune in technology from developing software without having a degree at all.

The important part is that the data scientist has to be able to think algorithmically, understand vectorized operations, and work with text files at the command line. If they don't have the skills, they can't possibly be a data scientist.

Math and Statistics Knowledge

A data scientist requires math and statistics knowledge to analyze data and extract insights. Without this knowledge, they don't know what methods or models to apply, so even if they've gotten the data into usable shape with their hacking skills, they can't move further than that.

While a PhD in statistics isn't required for a data scientist to be effective at what they do, they do need to be aware of how to develop and work with mathematical and statistical models. They must also be able to interpret the results.

Substantive Expertise

Substantive expertise refers to the fact that a data scientist must have knowledge of a particular field. In other words, they need to understand the subject matter and not just the technical side of things. This way, the data scientist can apply their other skills to the data so that they can achieve their objective. Essentially, this means that you want a data scientist in health care, for example, to have some health care experience and expertise. While this is not a prerequisite per se (data science tools can be applied to any problem), a data scientist should, at least, be willing to acquire the necessary domain knowledge when entering a new field.

All Three Skillsets Are Necessary

Only having two of these skills is not enough. For example, an excellent code hacker who knows math and statistics but has no substantive expertise might be great for ML, but it doesn't make them a data scientist.

Someone with substantive expertise and knowledge of math and statistics might be great for research, but they will not be a data scientist. Academia is mainly made up of people with these two skillsets.

The biggest problem starts when you have a person who is excellent with computers and has substantive expertise. It can actually make them dangerous. They know just enough to put together what looks like a legitimate analysis, but they don't understand how they reached their conclusions.

They have the skills to apply analytics to a problem. However, they don't have the theoretical foundation to ensure that they are doing the right thing. So, they might run a statistical test but could be using mistaken assumptions.

So, a competent data scientist needs to have all three skill sets, namely hacking, math and science knowledge, and substantive expertise.

What Motivates a Data Scientist?

If you want to manage data scientists effectively, you need to understand what motivates them. While each individual will have different motivations, data scientists share a variety of traits that can make them difficult to understand for people. This is because they have so many skills that it is difficult to put them in a particular box.

A data scientist isn't just a geek who knows math and statistics and can make computers sing. They also have outstanding communication and visualization skills, which means they can communicate effectively not only with senior management but also with clients and other stakeholders. It also makes some great storytellers, which can be vital in a business setting.

Data scientists are also curious about data and passionate about the business. They constantly want to improve and learn more, and while they might want to solve problems and influence things, they don't want authority. They tend to be strategic, proactive, creative, and innovative people who like to work with others.

Many of them need to be mentally stimulated, and solving problems is simply what they do. They are innately curious and are driven to grow, which often means that they love learning new things and expanding their skills.

So, when you think of what motivates a data scientist, you need to think beyond a paycheck. While a data scientist might come on board for great pay, they might not stay on board if they aren't being challenged or if they feel their work isn't being utilized effectively.

If you put your data scientist in a position in which they are doing a lot of repetitive work, their level of engagement will plummet, and you'll find them with one foot out the door.

In other words, if they have to spend inordinate amounts of time cleaning up data or performing any other task that is as exciting as watching paint dry, you are going to end up with someone who wants to leave your employment as quickly as they can.

Another concern is mental engagement. What we mean by this is if you ask them to solve problems that are simple and pose no challenge, they aren't going to appreciate it. That doesn't mean that you will always be able to provide them with challenges and that simple problems don't have to be solved. At the same time, though, consider that if you are hiring a data scientist, you should capitalize on their skill set.

After all, you wouldn't hire a rocket scientist to perform preventative maintenance on an airplane, would you? While he'd be fully capable of doing it, the concern is that, out of boredom, the rocket scientist will turn your plane into a spaceship.

Essentially, a rocket scientist will perform the preventative maintenance if required, but he won't do as good a job as he could for the simple reason that he's completely bored.

Hiring Data Scientists: What Does a Data Scientist Want?

There is a shortage of data scientists, but the demand is exceedingly high. Essentially, this high demand means that data scientists are in a position of power and can choose what projects to work on.

As an example, a somewhat decent data scientist working in London will be contacted by between 1 and 10 recruitment agents every week. So, to improve the odds of you hiring the right person, you need to be aware of what to offer them.

So, what does a data scientist want?

Good Compensation

The first thing you need to look at, of course, is compensation. Data scientists not only need money to live, like any human, but they also want to know that they are appreciated and are being compensated appropriately.

The Team

Some data scientists are more social than others and prefer working in teams where they are on the same wavelength as everybody else. This often means that they flourish in less formal cultures, though they might sometimes do better working from home. When someone has to spend lots of time thinking, a quiet environment at home might be more beneficial than an office space.

While you can't exactly change your entire company culture for one person, you can consider this preference and try to make some allowances to foster a better working relationship.

Types of Challenges

Data scientists thrive on challenge, though the type of challenge and/ or problem they are dealing with also matters. For example, some might prefer a particular field, such as health care or environmental issues, while others might prefer working on problems that affect society.

Another bias they might have could be related to the type of problem. For example, some data scientists prefer working on problems that encompass text data.

However, while these are just surface concerns, if you dig down, you often find that the key is that data scientists like to do and learn new things all the time.

The Technology Stack

The type of technology used will also play an important role because some data scientists will prefer working with systems they are already familiar with, while others want to give something new a go. One general trait that most data scientists share is that they don't want to work with legacy code and old technology.

While this will involve you talking to the data scientist in question, keep in mind that many of these people often like to learn new technologies. This could be simply because they want to better themselves, or because they enjoy the challenge, or because they want to earn better pay.

If you facilitate an environment where they can learn these new technologies, you stand a better chance of keeping them. However, don't forget that once they do expand their skill sets, you might have to increase their compensation accordingly to keep them on board.

The Academic Connection

Another way to motivate a data scientist is to provide them with funding for attending conferences. Many data scientists are closely connected to academia and have a habit of reading and/or writing papers, as well as going to conferences. This is a good thing for everyone because they keep their skills sharp and are always in the know about the latest advancements in data science.

Some of the top data science conferences a PhD-level data scientist will be interested in attending include:

- ICML—The International Conference on Machine Learning
- NeurIPS—Neural Information Processing Systems
- SIGKDD—ACM SIGKDD International Conference on Knowledge Discovery and Data Mining
- ECML-PKDD—European Conference on Machine Learning and Knowledge Discovery in Databases
- AI Stats

Change Your Hiring Mindset

When it comes to hiring a data scientist, you will have to change your mindset somewhat. Most employers take the same tack as they would when trying to fill any other role in their business. This usually means that they'll ask about a data scientist's experience in a specific field.

The problem with this is that data scientists often look to fields they haven't worked in before because they want to learn something new and avoid boredom. Working with data in a new area is far more interesting than doing the same thing over and over again.

Now, you might think that hiring a data scientist without experience in your field is a mistake. After all, you don't want to be the one funding a data scientist's education, do you?

Well, this is the precise wrong way to think about it because a data scientist isn't defined by the field they're experienced in but by their skill set, which is applicable to any field. As long as they have the tools, they can work in any domain, even if they've never seen it before.

Think of it like a dog trainer and behavioral specialist. While the trainer might work more frequently with Collies, for example, they are just as capable of training any other breed of dog, from English Bulldogs to Rottweilers. The tools and skills are the same, regardless of the breed they are working with.

Another problem is that employers don't always understand exactly what they're asking for. A frequent issue is that the human resources department will ask for someone with five years of experience in a particular technology, only to discover that the technology in question has only been around for two years, so it's not possible to have that much experience.

Therefore, it's generally a better idea to focus on the breadth of a data scientist's knowledge and skills rather than just experience.

Data scientists are often boxed into a field because employers don't understand how data scientists work and what their skill sets mean. So, a data scientist who has worked in finance, for example, would use tools such as predictive modeling and time series. These tools, however, aren't just limited to finance. They could be used just as effectively in other fields such as retail and health care.

The problem is that an employer will see how experienced the data scientist is with finances and assume that their skill set is only applicable to that particular field. This means that they could be missing out on a great opportunity to hire an outstanding data scientist.

In other words, you need to change your mindset when it comes to choosing the right person for the job because data scientists don't fit the usual mold.

Data Science Tribes

Data scientists can be categorized into large and small tribes based on how they became data scientists.

Unlike other professions, which usually involve the same path to become qualified, such as an accountant or a doctor, a person can become a data scientist in a variety of ways. Therefore, data scientists can be split into three major tribes and three minor tribes (Kampakis 2018b).

The major tribes are comprised of computer scientists, statisticians, and quantitative specialists from other fields.

The minor tribes can be separated into self-taught data scientists, software platform users, and domain specialists (Figure 4.1).

The Major Tribes

As previously stated, the three major tribes are computer scientists, statisticians, and other quantitative specialists. Let's take a closer look at each one.

Computer Scientists

Computer scientists have degrees in computer science, such as masters or PhDs in ML. The main benefit is that these types of data scientists are excellent at computer-related things such as coding, databases, and software. However, they often overlook traditional statistical techniques and theory, which are necessary or at least helpful in certain situations.

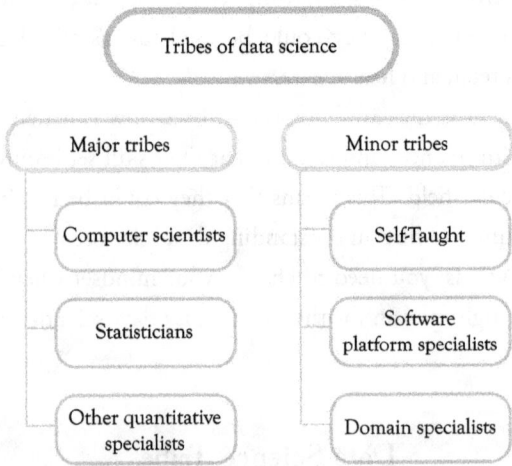

Figure 4.1 **The tribes of data scientists**

These types of data scientists are often a good option for ML tasks, like predictive modeling. They tend to have experience in Kaggle competitions, which is an excellent example of this type of problem.

Kaggle is a platform where people can engage in analytics and predictive modeling competitions, though it should be noted that Kaggle has joined Google Cloud ("The Beginner's Guide to Kaggle" 2017). Essentially, companies upload data sets, and then people compete to come up with the best possible model in terms of predicting and describing the data sets. It's an efficient way to discover the best approach for a specific predictive modeling task through crowdsourcing.

A computer scientist is a great option for small companies and start-ups because you can give them a data set for which you just want to find a good algorithm to predict something. They have excellent coding skills so they can easily integrate their work with the rest of platform.

They also have great database skills, which means that they can do a lot of data engineering work. Even if you have your own data engineers, it's still worth working with a computer scientist because it's easy for them to retrieve data and turn it into something usable, among other things.

It should be noted, though, that their lack of theoretical knowledge of statistics makes them inadequate for some situations, especially when you need research design.

Statisticians

Statisticians have degrees in statistics, as the name implies, or even in ML. However, while they have good theoretical knowledge, they rarely have the necessary coding or database skills.

Statisticians are your best option if you are interested in research design or statistical modeling. Therefore, if your goal is to discover the driving factors behind something or design an experiment, your best option is a statistician.

You also want to turn to a statistician if you're looking to model advanced complex problems while requiring a transparent modeling process.

Owing to their in-depth math and theory training, they are also effective at critiquing the work of other data scientists.

The main concern is that they generally have limited coding and database skills, which will lead to system integration issues. This will make the whole process more challenging and time-consuming.

Some statisticians are also inexperienced with predictive modeling, though the latter is more aligned with ML and rarely considered to be vital to statistics.

Check if they have any Kaggle experience and make sure that they have a minimum familiarity with ML concepts, such as cross-validation if you want to use their skills for predictive modeling.

Other Quantitative Specialists

The tribe of other quantitative specialists is comprised of people who come from fields that are heavy in math, such as physics, actuarial science, mathematics, econometrics, and so on. These specialists might also have degrees in statistics or ML.

These people are special because they frequently not only have a solid skillset but also provide creativity and out-of-the-box thinking, which is essential in data science. If the problem you're dealing with is in their field of expertise, then these are definitely people that you seriously need to consider hiring.

Of course, there is a drawback. Other quantitative specialists frequently lack effective training in ML or statistics, which can create issues in particular situations. Thus, it all depends on the person when it comes to quantitative specialists.

Owing to their lack of formal education in the field, you might have to do a little extra research to discover how effective they really are. Look for examples of their work on Kaggle or GitHub before you decide to hire them.

The fact that they're self-taught is not a criticism as many highly successful and effective people in the world are self-taught. It just means that you need to make sure that their skills are on the level you need them to be.

Other quantitative specialists tend to be people who have studied for one field and discovered that the money they can earn isn't all that great. Or, they had a lot of difficulty finding a good job. Then they discovered that data science pays really well, so they decided to branch out. For example, a chemist could decide to create a few mini-projects, upload them to GitHub, or enroll in a few competitions on Kaggle to find a job as a data scientist.

Personal experience shows that the most effective data scientists from this tribe are those who have trained to be physicists. This is because physics is full of applied math, which means that they can easily understand ML papers, since it's essentially the same type of math. Physicists also need to have some coding skills, which means that their skillset is often in line with what ML requires.

Other quantitative specialists will often be experts in their particular field, which could prove useful. For example, if your problem is related to econometrics, you might want to hire someone who is experienced in econometrics and has a little bit of ML knowledge.

The drawback is that some of these people will try to fake it. To get the job, they'll go through a few tutorials and online courses for a few weeks. Suddenly, they think they're a data scientist. You have to be very careful with these types of people because they can do significant damage to your project.

However, this in no way means that you shouldn't look at people who don't have a lot of experience. If they're honest about it and can show that they're smart and willing to learn, there's no reason not to give them a chance. Just make sure to put them in junior roles under more experienced supervision.

Convergence Point

All the tribes generally converge after about five or six years of experience. When someone has been working for a few years and they've taken part in between 10 and 30 projects, let's say, and they work in different fields for various companies, they end up developing a significant range of skills. A PhD is just an added bonus.

At this point, they've done some coding and picked up all sorts of skills and knowledge. They're also quite aware of what's available, in terms of methods and techniques. Even if they don't know how to implement them, they still know how a problem should be solved and will know who to speak to in order to get the work done. Sometimes, it's not as important to have the skill yourself, but to be aware of your limits and to know what solutions are available and how to get to the people who can implement them.

When you find a person like this with a lot of experience across the board, you don't really want to concern yourself with their background. What they've learned over the years is more important, as well as whether they have the skills and awareness to help you.

The problem is that some people might look like they have a lot of experience but it's actually limited. They may have worked on the same one or two projects for multiple years. While they are very experienced, it's only in a narrow niche. These aren't the people we're referring to.

The people we're referring to have been proactive in learning new things, such as becoming more experienced with R, or Python, they've done a little research design, and so on.

The Small Tribes

The small or minor tribes are less populated and those included here tend not to be data scientists but people with analytical skills. The three minor tribes are the self-taught, the software platform specialist, and the domain specialist.

Self-taught people have usually studied an unrelated, random field, though, in some cases, it might be software development. They may have taken part in a few Kaggle competitions and that's the limit of their experience.

While other quantitative specialists encompassed in the larger tribes might be self-taught in certain respects, their field of study has already provided them with some skills that can easily translate to data science.

In this case, we're talking about someone who's studied art history, for example. They then discover that there aren't a lot of professional opportunities in their field, and they decide to become a data scientist.

Then there's the software platform specialist. They just know how to use that specific tool and they can offer a lot of value for money if you only have a simple problem to solve. If all you're looking for is some reporting, for example, then this type of person is your best bet because they'll offer the best value for money.

You also don't have to be concerned about them getting bored, like you would if you tried to get someone who has a PhD in deep learning to do the same thing.

However, you can't turn to them for more complicated problems because you will end up in that danger zone we discussed earlier in the chapter. Without a proper background in math and statistics, they'll only be able to apply the tool in certain situations, and they definitely aren't people you want building models or predictive tools.

The domain specialist is someone with extensive ML knowledge but only in a specific niche. One example is someone who specializes in deep learning and computer vision. They might have done undergrad work or hold a master's degree or PhD in computer vision.

If your problem is related to computer vision, then they are definitely the best option. However, if you have a different type of problem, these aren't the people you want to turn to. While it won't be hard for them to pick up new skills, it will take some time.

Like the software platform specialist, domain specialists can also fall into the danger zone. They'll believe that the skills they already have can be applied to any problem, even if that's not the case.

As previously mentioned, though, you should be open to people who know their limitations and want to expand their skill sets. These are the people who know it will take them a few months to learn the particulars of any field, but they are more than willing to do the work and put in the effort. Sometimes this is the best approach because you'll gain a very loyal data scientist since not many companies are willing to support people when it comes to improving themselves.

Building a Data-Centric Culture

When it comes to a data-centric culture, you need to look at it on three levels.

At the **management level**, it's all about using logic and data to drive decision making rather than your gut.

In an organization with a data science culture, at the management level, your gut should not be making an appearance unless you're at lunch. It's also about being data driven and data informed.

At the **employee level**, it's about hiring data scientists and managing them effectively. You need to find the right people and create a friendly environment for them.

At the **organizational level**, building the right culture means mixing together the right elements from the management and employee levels. The result is a data-centric organization. You will then be able to maximize the effectiveness of data science from the beginning data collection stages all the way to application. At this point, you'll start seeing real benefits.

Understanding the Concepts of Data Informed and Data Driven

Data informed means that a person or organization is using data and the context of data in their conversation and decision-making processes. If someone is using dashboards and KPIs (Key Performance Indicators), they are data informed (Kampakis 2018a).

Being data driven, though, means taking things to the next level. This is when you start applying smarter and more complex algorithms and methodologies to acquire and analyze the data. It also means more advanced decision-making processes because you either rely completely on the algorithm to make the decision, or you at least consider the algorithm's conclusions.

Most companies should try to get to the data-driven stage. Once there, you can rely on data and data science to help you when it comes to making disruptive decisions. In some situations, data science could completely replace human decision making.

Being data driven doesn't necessarily mean that the algorithm has to make every decision, but it does mean that you use algorithmic outputs in the decision-making process throughout at least part of the organization.

The advantage is that your organization will become far more efficient, and your decision-making process will also be more effective. A recommender system, for example, will make better decisions than a human in terms of what a return customer might like or want (Kampakis 2019).

There's also the consideration of scale. If you want to scale up, like Amazon, you aren't going to be able to manually make recommendations. Instead, you're going to have to rely on an algorithm.

However, keep in mind that if you don't use data the right way, you can end up making poor decisions that lead to expensive and incorrect actions.

The problem is that if you're not using data the right way, and you don't have the right theory, or you didn't run the right tests, you end up making the wrong decisions. Even worse, you're completely confident in those decisions because you believe you used an effective scientific approach.

The easiest way to overcome this problem is to employ data scientists who know what they're doing. Of course, you also need to have the right culture to allow the scientists to interact with other divisions effectively.

What Does a Data-Centric Organization Look Like?

First, you have a 360-degree view of what is happening when it comes to data and data science. Data science is its own division, which means the scientist is free to explore new things, even if they might create disruptions.

The data scientist also has more responsibility, which can be motivating but can also be risky. Since you have a complete view of the situation, though, you can reduce the risk.

You also have effective reporting and communication channels between all the essential departments, especially when it comes to the developers and data scientists, but also between the data scientists and management.

This is vital because the work the data scientist does should have an impact. However, you also need to know what data is being collected, how it's being used, and how it's all being implemented.

It's essential to be aware in terms of data collection because there are legal issues regarding data privacy, which means you need to know exactly how data is being collected and used.

You also need to know what the data scientist is working on and to ensure that it is being implemented and used positively in your organization. It's essential to have effective communication channels because then different divisions can scrutinize the work of others to ensure that the work being carried out is relevant to the organization.

How to Build a Data Science Culture

This first step to building a data science culture is determining why you need data science. Three common scenarios exist in business:

1. Data science is a vital part of your business, maybe you work in robotics, or your organization is tech-focused in some way. In this case, you probably have the knowledge to do it yourself.
2. You want to improve the efficiency of the company you run.
3. You might want to improve sales, so you're looking for a good recommender system or other tools and/or algorithms that can help.

Once you understand why you need data science, you'll be able to determine what your next step should be. You will encounter problems, though, and one of these is resistance to change.

Resistance to Change

Smaller firms and start-ups tend to be more flexible, so resistance to change won't be much of an issue if you fall into this category. However, if you are a big organization, you might have a few problems.

You'll find that there are three types of resistance to change, namely cultural, personal, and intellectual.

Cultural resistance to change is when you have a big and traditional organization with multiple layers of management that don't really see the value of data science. Or, you're operating in a field that doesn't have much to do with math, data, and statistics, so selling the rest of the firm on the idea will be a challenge.

Personal resistance to change can happen in smaller companies as well as big ones, and that's when you have employees who don't like to change on a personal level.

This frequently happens when the employees simply don't see any benefit from changing. They don't see the advantages of doing anything, such as exporting a database or trying to implement an algorithm.

Intellectual resistance to change occurs when people are afraid of what they don't understand. Many people are still concerned about artificial intelligence (AI) because they worry we will end up facing a situation like in Terminator where Skynet took over the world.

Intellectual resistance to change tends to be infrequent in organizations because most people understand that data can be useful in improving efficiency and sales. However, if you find that there is some intellectual resistance to change, a good solution is to hire a data officer. This person can own the data and show people how effective and useful it can be.

The Journey to Change

The first step in your journey to change involves determining how data scientists will get you to your destination. This requires creating an environment that's friendly to data science where scientists can talk about it and attempt to carry out projects that have significant impact.

While change might be slow, it will help if people can see results. They'll understand the benefits and will become more willing to adopt something new.

Finding someone to champion the whole process is also essential. A champion can create enthusiasm and bring everyone else on board. Your champion has to be a high-ranking employee who really believes in the new approach. They also have to be popular and someone that your employees will listen to, regardless of what they're saying.

How to Start

You can implement a data science culture either with baby steps or on a use-case basis.

If you're going to start with baby steps, that means collecting tons of data and ensuring the decision makers learn about data science. Then, you'll use simple graphs and stats, which means you will become more data informed. The next step will be to hire someone to provide further insights from the data.

The use-case approach is more top-down and occurs when the organization has a particular problem that they need solved. They might start by employing someone to help with the design of a plan and to come up with a solution for their specific problem. Then, they look at how the findings are relevant to other situations.

Where to Start

The first step is to map how your organization uses data. You need to be aware of how data flows within your organization, from when it's collected all the way to how it's used.

You want to get your employees to understand how important strategy and innovation are while rewarding good behavior, which is essential for data scientists. They often want recognition and to feel as if they're making a difference. So, promote good work and show others how effective your data scientists are.

You also want to create an embedded culture, as this is the most effective way to break down silos and improve communication. Your data scientists must work closely with developers, product owners, managers, and other stakeholders. This is essential to ensuring that research is relevant, results are implemented, and they have a positive effect within the firm.

Key Takeaways

- There are different types of data scientists. The main ones are: the ML specialist, the statistician, and the quantitative specialist.
- Integrating data scientists within an organization requires the right culture.
- Creating the right culture requires overcoming resistance to change. Some organizations prefer to focus on small projects first, and others prefer a more disruptive approach.

CHAPTER 5

An Introduction to Blockchain

Blockchain is a decentralized, digital ledger that is used to record transactions across many computers so that the records cannot be altered retroactively without the alteration of all subsequent blocks and the collusion of the network.

Since the seminal paper by Satoshi Nakamoto (2008), blockchain has risen as one of the most important trends in technology with applications ranging from finance, to supply chains, and more.

In this chapter, we'll be exploring everything a nontechnical decision maker needs to know about blockchain. We'll start with the history of money, and how this incentivized the creation of blockchain technology, before moving on to other types of application (Figure 5.1).

The Evolution of Money and Payment Systems

Commerce has been around for a very long time, even before money, as we know it today, came into being. Remember that commerce is defined as the exchange of goods, services, or something of value between entities.

Therefore, people weren't exchanging goods or services for money when commerce first came about. Instead, other forms of payment were used.

Of course, since then, money and payment systems have changed significantly. Instead of exchanging livestock, for example, we use things such as credit cards and cryptocurrency. In other words, we can pay for things anytime we like, no matter where we are.

So, let's look at how money and payment systems evolved from the very beginning.

1991	2009	2011	2014	2017
Blockchain idea was presented by Stuart Harver and W. Scott Stornetta	First bitcoin transaction took place between Hal Finney and Satoshi Nakamoto	Bitcoin reached parity with the U.S. dollar	Kevin McCoy mined the first known NFT quantum	MarkerDAO, oldest DeFi project, was launched

2008	2010	2013	2015	2021
Satoshi Nakamoto released a white paper with bitcoin's blockchain	First bitcoin purchase was made. 10,000 BTC for a pizza	Vitalik Buterin published a white paper on Ethereum	Ethereum entered the market NASDAQ commits to a blockchain trail	"EVERYDAYS: THE FIRST 5000 DAYS" sold at Christie's for $69.3m A CyptoPunk NFT bought for $532m by the seller facebook rebranded itself as meta

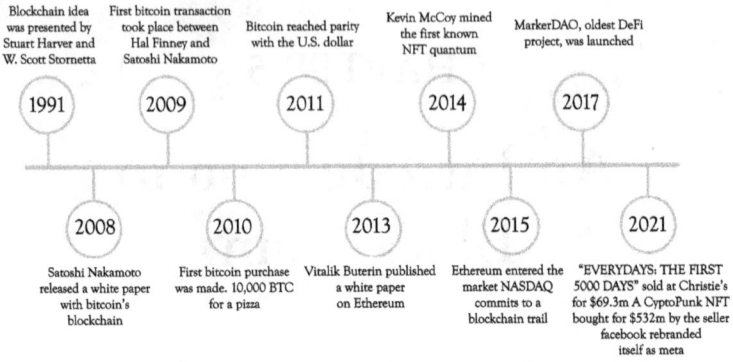

Figure 5.1 A history of blockchain

Bartering

Commerce first started with bartering, which simply means that people would exchange goods and services for other goods and services. For example, a farmer might need a hoe to till his field. He'd go to the blacksmith and offer to pay with the vegetables he cultivated. Both parties benefited since the farmer would get the hoe while the blacksmith would get food in exchange.

At the time, livestock was considered a measure of wealth. The more cows, or sheep you owned, the wealthier you were, which is why livestock was often used to barter for goods and services.

Coins

One problem with bartering was that it could be complicated. You had to plan out what you needed and transport the goods in advance. So instead, some ancient civilizations would use beads and shells as a form of payment, making them the original coins.

The advantage was portability. It was easier to carry shells and beads than heavy goods. They would act as an IOU, so people could get what they needed right away.

Eventually, precious metals replaced beads and shells as they had inherent value. In other words, it was no longer an IOU because the coin itself had value due to the precious metal it was made of.

Among the first recorded uses of gold and silver coins is attributed to the people of the ancient civilization of Lydia.

Leather as Currency

In ancient China, people used white deerskin as currency. The principle was similar to the cash we use today, but the "notes" were much larger. In fact, this money could have been as big as one square foot of leather.

Paper Money

Initially developed by the Chinese, paper money had a problem. It was difficult to figure out its value and maintain it. Other problems included not only the production process but also inflation. So, paper money eventually fell out of use. In fact, it came and went throughout ancient history because of its challenges.

Gold

In 1816, England set gold as a standard of value. Subsequently, Europe began to use gold as a standard to measure the value of banknotes. In other words, each banknote was worth a particular amount of gold. However, it should be noted that to issue a banknote for a certain amount of gold, the bank had to have the equivalent amount of gold in their reserves.

In 1900, the United States adopted the same standard. Then, in 1913, the Federal Reserve system was established. Among other things, the Federal Reserve had to ensure that checks and notes could be converted for gold and would always be honored.

Credit Cards

The 20th century saw the rise of the credit card. It initially started with retailers offering consumers credit, including department stores and gas stations. They created cards that would make it easier for people to spend money.

The U.S. Dollar

In 1933, deflation was a severe problem that was only getting worse in the United States. Therefore, the country did away with the gold standard so Americans wouldn't exchange their banknotes for gold and deplete the gold supply.

From that point on, the Federal government officially backed the monetary system, though the United States would allow foreign governments to trade in their dollars for gold until 1971. This practice was ended over the concern that the U.S. gold supply would dwindle.

Online Payment Systems

The 1990s saw the rise of the Internet, which naturally led to many people shopping online. As a result, a wide range of payment systems arose that enabled people to pay for their online purchases. Evidence suggests that one of the first companies to perform an online transaction was Pizza Hut because people could order via their website as far back as 1994.

Mobile Payments

As more and more people used mobiles, mobile payment systems developed. The first transaction was registered in 1997 and is owed to Coca-Cola and their special vending machines that allowed consumers to pay via text message.

Since then, mobile has become one of the most popular forms of payment. People can pay at any time, regardless of where they are, and merchants can receive payments without needing a cash register or traditional POS.

The Rise of Bitcoin and Blockchain

The idea of blockchain, also known as distributed ledger technology (DLT), has been around for quite a while. In fact, it was first presented by Stuart Haber and W. Scott Stornetta in 1991 (Beyer 2018). However, it wasn't until 2008, when Satoshi Nakamoto released a white paper with Bitcoin's blockchain, that certain challenges were solved, and the practical applications became obvious (Nakamoto 2008).

No one knows who Satoshi Nakamoto is as the name is a pseudonym. Many suspect that the pseudonym represents a group rather than being one person.

Blockchain is what makes Bitcoin possible, and we can't really talk about one without talking about the other. This technology has developed by leaps and bounds since 2008 and has the potential to affect every industry.

Essentially, blockchain is a large electronic system that allows you to build applications, with currency being just one of them. Interestingly, it wasn't until around 2014 that people realized the technology behind Bitcoin could be used for many other things.

In essence, blockchain consists of a transparent and decentralized ledger that makes a permanent record of a transaction between two people without the need for another party to authenticate it. The result is a highly efficient process that significantly lowers transaction costs.

When companies realized how powerful blockchain was, many began investing in and exploring the technology to understand its full potential. Though we haven't yet scratched the surface, blockchain has already proven that it can affect everything from supply chains and health care to contract management and voting.

Around 2013, Vitalik Buterin, the cofounder of Bitcoin magazine, became frustrated with Bitcoin's limitations and pushed for a more flexible blockchain. However, the Bitcoin community didn't agree. So, Buterin went on to develop the second public blockchain, which he called Ethereum.

The biggest difference between Ethereum and Bitcoin is that the former can record other transactions such as contracts and loans, whereas the Bitcoin blockchain is dedicated to currency.

Ethereum came to market in 2015, and people can use it to create smart contracts. Furthermore, these smart contracts can be automatically processed based on various conditions set within the blockchain.

At the moment, the key driver of blockchain is the "proof of work" concept. Essentially, a very complicated and expensive computer calculation is done (a process referred to as "mining") to create a block, which consists of multiple transactions.

Subsequently, the miners will verify the legitimacy of the transactions within the block by solving a proof of work problem. Once again, these problems are very complicated and require a lot of computing power to solve, making them extremely expensive.

The first miner who finds the solution is provided with a reward, and the transaction is saved on the blockchain.

Interestingly, Ethereum developers want to switch to a more accessible consensus system referred to as "proof of stake."

The goal is to verify transactions and reach a consensus on the blockchain. However, the process differs in that the new block's creator is selected using a deterministic approach, "depending on its wealth, also defined as a stake" ("Proof-of-Stake (PoS)" n.d.).

The miners, known as foragers, don't receive a reward. Instead, they earn transaction fees. Some support the shift due to the lower cost required to obtain a distributed type of consensus.

What Is Blockchain?

As previously explained, blockchain consists of a decentralized ledger of permanent records within a network where information is stored. It's a distributed database stored digitally on multiple computers.

What makes blockchain special is that it ensures the validity and safety of the recorded data and, therefore, establishes trust without the need to get a third party involved.

The difference between a traditional database and blockchain lies in how the data is structured. In a blockchain, the data is organized in groups, referred to as blocks. Each block can only hold a certain amount of data, after which it is closed and connected to the block that was filled before it, creating a data chain known as the blockchain.

Any new data collected after a block has been closed and added to the chain is stored in a new block, which will also be closed and added to the chain when filled.

The advantage of this approach is that it creates a timeline that can't be tampered with, especially when it is implemented in a decentralized way. For example, when a block is full, it can no longer be altered and is added to the chain with a timestamp.

While a blockchain can store all sorts of information, it has primarily been used as a transaction ledger, such as with Bitcoin.

When it comes to Bitcoin, blockchain technology has been applied using a decentralized approach, meaning that a single person or group can't control it. Instead, all the people on the blockchain maintain collective control.

Furthermore, a decentralized blockchain is immutable, meaning that the data cannot be changed, deleted, or destroyed, making it irreversible.

In essence, the idea of using blockchain is to allow people who don't trust each other to share important data securely and so that it cannot be tampered with.

Understanding How Blockchain Works

Blockchain is made up of three vital elements: blocks, nodes, and miners.

As previously explained, every chain consists of multiple blocks. However, every block contains data, a nonce, and a hash.

The nonce is a 32-bit whole number that is generated randomly when the block is created. The nonce then creates a block header hash, which is a 256-bit number connected to the nonce.

So, when the first block in a chain is created, the attached nonce spawns the cryptographic hash. The data that is then registered within that block will forever be connected to the nonce and hash.

Miners create new blocks on the blockchain, with each block featuring a unique nonce and hash. However, every block also references the hash of the block before it, which makes mining difficult, especially on a large chain.

The way mining works is that special software is used to solve very complicated math problems that allow miners to find a nonce that can generate an acceptable hash. Considering that a nonce is 32 bits and a hash is 256, there are approximately 4 billion combinations, and only one is correct. When a miner finds the right combination, their block is added to the chain.

If anyone wants to change an earlier block in the chain, they also have to mine all the subsequent blocks. This is why it's tough to tamper with blockchain technology. While it is possible, it is prohibitively expensive and requires a lot of time and computing power to the point where it's simply not worth it.

When a miner successfully mines a block, meaning that they found the right nonce and hash, all the nodes on the network accept the change, and the miner receives a financial reward.

Nodes are any form of electronic device that can maintain a copy of the blockchain and ensure that network continues to function.

Every node has a copy of the blockchain. The network must approve the new block for the chain to be updated. Every action on the blockchain can easily be viewed and verified, and each participant is provided with a unique number that shows what transactions they performed.

By combining easily accessible and transparent information with an accountability system, the blockchain can maintain its integrity and ensure trustworthy transactions between people (Figure 5.2).

Cryptography and Blockchain

When it comes to blockchain, cryptography ensures that the transactions and participants are secure. It also ensures that operations can be independent of a central authority while also providing protection against double-spending.

For a long time, the concept of double-spending was a major issue with cryptocurrencies. The idea of double-spending is that a unit of cryptocurrency could be spent twice since digital information is relatively easy to duplicate by someone who knows what they're doing. Thanks to how blockchain works, this is no longer a concern.

So, how does cryptography work in terms of blockchain?

Cryptography allows people to send messages that are secured to each other. The person sending the message uses a key and an algorithm to

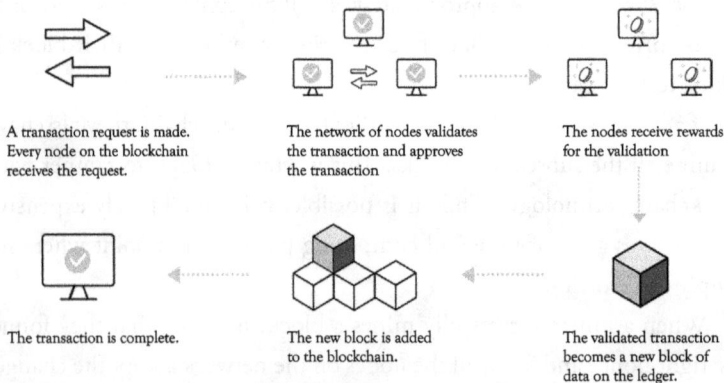

A transaction request is made. Every node on the blockchain receives the request.

The network of nodes validates the transaction and approves the transaction

The nodes receive rewards for the validation

The transaction is complete.

The new block is added to the blockchain.

The validated transaction becomes a new block of data on the ledger.

Figure 5.2 How blockchain works

encrypt their data. They then send the message to the other participant. The person receiving the message decrypts it, using the right key and algorithm, so they can see the original data.

The encryption key is the most critical part of cryptography because it makes the message, transaction, or data unreadable for a person who is not authorized to see it. It can only be processed by the person who was meant to receive the message.

While Bitcoin doesn't specifically use this type of cryptography to hide the transactions, the transactions are still anonymous because there is no need to supply personal information.

For example, all you have to do is open a cryptocurrency wallet, and you are assigned a public and a private key. You don't have to supply any personal information because all the transactions are already trusted as they are being conducted through the blockchain.

Some of the cryptography methods used for cryptocurrencies include symmetric encryption cryptography, asymmetric encryption cryptography, and hashing.

Symmetric Encryption Cryptography

In symmetric encryption cryptography, the same key is used to encrypt and decrypt the message. The advantage of this form of encryption is that it's simple to implement and requires little operational overhead. However, the drawbacks include challenges with scaling and problems with keeping the shared key secure.

Asymmetric Encryption Cryptography

With asymmetric encryption cryptography, two different keys are used for the encryption and decryption of the data. One key is public, and it can be shared openly, such as the address of your wallet. Conversely, only the owner knows the private key.

In this case, the message will be encrypted using the public key, but only the recipient's private key can decrypt it.

This encryption approach helps not only with encryption but also authentication. In terms of authentication, the public key checks the related private key for the actual sender. When it comes to encryption, only the person holding the correct private key can decrypt the message.

Hashing

Hashing efficiently verified the transaction data's integrity on the network. It ensures that no tampering occurs with the structure of the data on the blockchain and encodes account addresses. It makes mining possible and is a vital component in the encryption of transactions that take place between accounts.

Discover the Different Types of Blockchain Technology

Currently, there are four primary types of blockchain networks: public, private, consortium or federated, and hybrid. Each of these has pros and cons, with some being better suited for certain applications than others.

Espae Hong, the head of CBDC Blockchain Research Institute, explains, "While the blockchain technology behind projects is the same, the target end-users of the different types of blockchain may differ." Public blockchains, for example, are aimed at the general public, as the name implies. Conversely, private blockchain networks are designed for "invitation-only users and their networks" (Parizo n.d.).

Public Blockchain

The public blockchain allowed the creation of Bitcoin and helped make DLT popular. This type of network eliminates issues inherent to centralization, such as reduced security and minimal transparency.

With DLT, the data isn't stored in a single place but distributed across a peer-to-peer network, which is where the name comes from.

However, since it is decentralized, there must be a way to verify that the data is authentic, which is where the consensus algorithm we already discussed comes in. Essentially, the network's participants come to an agreement in terms of what state the ledger is currently in with proof of work and proof of stake consensus methods, among others.

A public blockchain has no restrictions and doesn't require any permissions, which means that anyone with access to the Internet can join the platform and act as a node. This person can view current and past data, as well as conduct mining activities.

Data or transactions that have been validated cannot be changed, though anyone can verify said transactions, identify bugs, or suggest changes as the code tends to be open source.

Advantages

One major advantage of public blockchains is that they are independent. It doesn't matter what organization or which person started it. As long as there are devices still connected to the network, the blockchain will continue to operate, even if the founding organization (or person) no longer exists.

Some public blockchains provide rewards to encourage users to commit the computing power necessary to keep the network up and running.

Public blockchains are also transparent, meaning that anyone on the network can view the data. Furthermore, these networks are also largely secure, as long as people are strict about following protocols.

Disadvantages

Like with anything, public blockchains also have certain disadvantages. For example, it can be quite slow considering the amount of "work" that goes into verifying a transaction.

Furthermore, an organization cannot limit access or usage. The problem is that a bad actor who gains 51 percent or more of the network's computing power can change it however they like.

Another problem with a public blockchain is that it can be challenging to scale. As more devices join the network, it slows down until it's pretty much crawling.

Use Cases

Public blockchains are used mainly for the mining and exchange of cryptocurrencies, such as Bitcoin. However, these networks also shine in situations where a clear chain of custody is required, such as public records of ownership and notarization of affidavits.

This type of network is also a good option for organizations that are fully transparent, such as nongovernmental organizations and other social support groups. They are not recommended for private businesses.

Private Blockchain

A private blockchain consists of a network controlled by a single entity or that functions in a restricted environment. Though it operates as a public blockchain in terms of decentralization and using a peer-to-peer network, a private blockchain is much smaller.

Furthermore, users must be invited to join the network because it's usually set up inside an organization. These types of networks are also known as enterprise or permissioned blockchains.

Advantages

A private blockchain is, in essence, like a company's internal network. It's the equivalent of an intranet, where public blockchains are the equivalent of the Internet.

Thus, the company that controls the private blockchain can do the same things as it does with a traditional network, including setting permission levels, authorizations, security, and accessibility.

So, a company could allow only specific nodes to see, edit, or add data, while others would only be able to see the data. The organization can also restrict access so other parties would only be able to view certain data.

A big advantage of private blockchains is that they're very fast because they're so small. Therefore, they can complete transactions much faster than a public blockchain.

Disadvantages

Some claim that private blockchains can't be called true blockchains because the whole idea is of decentralization without a single entity in control. Trust is also a problem because a central node determines what is and isn't valid.

Security can also be an issue because there are fewer nodes, and if some of them turn out to be bad actors, the whole consensus method becomes null and void. The proprietary code backing these blockchains can also cause security issues because it can't be audited or confirmed by independent users.

Use Cases

Private blockchains are so fast that they are perfect for situations where the network must be secured cryptographically, but the organization doesn't want the public to access their information. They can be used for things such as managing trade secrets, auditing, managing supply chains, internal voting, and asset ownership.

Hybrid Blockchain

As the name implies, hybrid blockchains feature private and public blockchain elements. Thus, organizations can create a private, permission-based blockchain with a public system that doesn't require permissions. This way, the company can create a network that establishes what data will be publicly available and who can access what data.

Though data stored in a hybrid blockchain is usually not public, it can be verified when necessary. Just like with a public blockchain, transactions registered in the blockchain cannot be altered.

Furthermore, while joining the blockchain provides users with full access, their identity is protected until they conduct a transaction. Only then will their identity be revealed, and only to the other person involved in the transaction.

Advantages

Since hybrid blockchains operate in a closed environment, it's not possible for bad actors to take over 51 percent of the network, making it highly secure. It is one of the biggest advantages of this type of blockchain.

It also ensures privacy but allows communication with third parties. Hybrid blockchains also scale better than public ones while still providing the same cheap but often faster transactions.

Disadvantages

Hybrid blockchains don't have the same level of transparency as public ones because the controlling entity can hide information. It's also difficult to upgrade because users don't really have a reason to support or grow the network since there is no real incentive.

Use Cases

Hybrid blockchain is great for a number of applications, especially in fields like real estate. For example, a realtor can not only set up a hybrid blockchain that runs their internal, private systems but also shows the public specific information, like property listings, ensuring the work doesn't have to be done twice.

This blockchain can also help retailers streamline processes and can even help companies in highly regulated markets. It's a great option for health care, as patient records can be stored, and permissions can be applied so that only the health care provider and the patient can see the data.

The government can also use hybrid blockchains for citizens' private data, which can be securely stored and shared between institutions on this type of network.

Consortium or Federated Blockchain

A consortium or federated blockchain is somewhat similar to a hybrid blockchain because it encompasses elements from private and public blockchains. However, unlike the hybrid version, where there's a single controlling entity, the federated blockchain is made up of multiple organizations that work together on the network. As there are numerous players involved, it significantly reduces all the risks associated with a single entity being in control.

The consensus process is controlled by predetermined nodes. The blockchain features a specific node that opens, receives, and validates transactions, called a validator node. The other nodes on the network can initiate or receive transactions.

Advantages

The advantage of federated blockchains is that they feature a higher level of security than public blockchains. They're also more efficient and scale better. Organizations can also control access, determining who can see specific data.

Disadvantages

Once again, the issue of transparency arises. The moment one can restrict access to data, then it can no longer be called transparent.

Additionally, while federated blockchains are more secure than public blockchains, they are still susceptible to attack via member nodes. Another problem is that regulations of the blockchain itself can actually hurt the functionality of the network in the event of an attack.

Use Cases

Federated blockchains are great options for industries such as banking and research. For example, a number of banks or research organizations can come together to create a federated blockchain. They'll decide on the validator nodes and create an environment that allows for much faster and cheaper processing of transactions.

Blockchain Implementations

When most people hear of blockchain, they automatically think of cryptocurrencies. And that's natural, seeing that Bitcoin was pretty much the first application of the technology and the one that is most famous.

However, that is not the only implementation, so let's take a look at some specific applications of blockchains in the real world.

Bitcoin

While the concept of blockchain had been around for a while, it was only in 2009 when Bitcoin launched that the technology gained a real-world application.

The Bitcoin digital currency is built on blockchain, and, as a result, it offers people a faster and cheaper way of completing transactions with each other. Other benefits include anonymity and lack of a central authority, which is what attracts many people to digital currency.

Ethereum

Ethereum was developed as a reaction to the limitations of Bitcoin. Essentially, this platform expands on Bitcoin, even though it has its own digital currency known as Ether. Instead of being focused just on currency, though, the platform allows users to build a variety of applications. It also has its own programming language known as Solidity.

It's far more flexible than Bitcoin, which is likely why it's so popular. The network's users can not only create, publish, and use applications but they can also monetize them, which is, essentially, the incentive to participate and maintain the network.

Hyperledger Foundation

The Hyperledger Foundation is an open-source community where developers create various frameworks, libraries, and tools for private, hybrid, and federated blockchains designed for use by enterprises.

It brings together people from all over the world, including financial, banking, IoT, supply chain, manufacturing, and tech leaders.

The idea is that a permissioned blockchain is very different from a public blockchain such as Bitcoin or Ethereum. Therefore, the Hyperledger Foundation works toward ensuring that enterprises have the tools they need to apply blockchain effectively not only within their own companies but also across organizations.

As laid out on their website, the Hyperledger Foundation's goals include:

- Creating enterprise-grade, open-source ledger frameworks and code bases that will support effective business transactions.
- Providing an infrastructure that's neutral, open, and community-driven while also being subject to business and technical governance.
- Develop blockchain and shared ledger POCs, field trials, deployments, and use cases by building a powerful community.
- Teach people about the benefits of blockchain and the potential applications in the market.

The InterPlanetary File System (IPFS)

The InterPlanetary File System (IPFS) is a peer-to-peer storage network. Essentially, instead of people having to connect to a server to see a website, they connect to their peers, where the information is stored in a distributed fashion.

The goal with IPFS is to make the Internet faster, safer, more open, and more resilient. With IPFS, you no longer need to rely on a hosting provider for your website. Instead, it will be distributed across the network.

Corda

Corda is a DLT designed for businesses. It allows participants to store transactions so that they don't need to constantly check that their books are aligned. It also reduces the need for every participant on the network to view every transaction because only the people involved are interested in the information.

For example, if a bank sends money from a client account to another account at a different bank, both the sending and the receiving bank must verify that the transfer was valid. They must also check that the funds were not only sent correctly but also appropriately received.

To make sure that the money in one account is reduced by the right amount while the money in the receiving account is increased correctly means both banks have to conduct multiple checks. Basically, they need to make sure the money wasn't magically created and that it doesn't vanish into thin air. Another issue is that some of the checks are manual, making the whole process incredibly time-consuming.

With Corda, this reconciliation could be completely eliminated because a transaction can only be committed when all the parties confirm that the inputs and outputs are correct. The transaction won't go through if someone is not in agreement.

Nonfungible Tokens (NFTs)

A nonfungible token or NFT is an irreplaceable crypto asset, making it unique, and it is a representation of a digital or nondigital asset. Some of the underlying assets can be:

- Collectibles
- GIFs
- Music
- Animation
- Video
- Signatures
- Car deed
- Legal documents

Conversely, Bitcoin is fungible, which means you can trade one Bitcoin for another and still have the same thing.

What makes NFTs so popular is that only one person can own them at a time. Ownership is determined by a unique ID and other data, while ownership and transfer are managed via smart contracts. So, you can prove ownership that is authenticated by a digital token on the blockchain.

Many creators are taking advantage of NFTs because they allow other people to invest in them. They're also used as a speculative asset, with people buying NFTs to hold on to until their value increases.

Ethereum was the first blockchain to support NFTs. It has a system called ERC-721, which allows for the creation of unique tokens on the Ethereum blockchain. Since then, many other blockchains have come to support NFTs like Solana and Tezos.

Decentralized Finance

Decentralized finance is a new form of finance that is emerging in the world. It is a type of financial system that does not rely on centralized authorities to manage transactions.

Some well-known examples are shown below.

Uniswap

Launched in 2018, Uniswap is a cryptocurrency exchange based on the Ethereum blockchain. It is a decentralized cryptocurrency exchange, making it different from the more mainstream exchanges that exist such as Binance and Coinbase. These are examples of centralized exchanges, so there is a single entity or company that operates and controls the exchange.

With Uniswap, there is no central controlling authority. This means the buying and selling of cryptocurrencies like Bitcoin takes place on a blockchain using smart contracts.

Curve Finance

Curve Finance is another decentralized exchange running on the Ethereum blockchain. The main difference between Curve Finance and Uniswap is that Curve Finance specifically focuses on stablecoins. Stablecoins are still cryptocurrencies, but their price is linked to another financial instrument, such as a mainstream currency, another cryptocurrency, or a commodity.

Many people also use Curve Finance to swap tokens to something different that has a similar price. Curve Finance is used for this because of its favorable pricing formula.

Yearn Finance

Yearn Finance is a suite of tools that people use to optimize their crypto assets and maximize their returns. The tools primarily facilitate trading and lending and, as the platform is decentralized, they remove the need for an intermediary.

AAVE

AAVE is a decentralized finance platform that allows users to lend and borrow cryptocurrencies. As it is decentralized, there are no intermediaries involved in the lending or borrowing process.

Borrowers on AAVE must first allocate collateral to the platform. They can then only borrow up to the amount that they have on AAVE. Those lending on AAVE earn interest, plus they are fully in control of how much they lend.

The Metaverse

The metaverse is what people are calling the Internet of the future that will consist of virtual worlds connected to each other. These virtual worlds will allow users to connect to them using augmented or virtual reality interfaces and share experiences with others. They will allow for a much greater level of immersion.

And blockchains will be a crucial component of the success of the metaverse. They will allow for things such as virtual currencies, game creation, and play, NFTs that will allow people to own items in the virtual world, and much more.

More importantly, blockchain will ensure that all the data in the metaverse is secure and protected. When you consider that the goal is for people to live part of their lives in this virtual world, protecting people's information will be more important than ever.

Some popular metaverse projects are the following:

Decentraland

Decentraland has been in development since 2015, but it only became publicly available in 2020. It is essentially a virtual world that users can access through their browser. Users can make purchases, such as buying plots of virtual land, with the transactions being processed either through NFTs (which represent the plots of land) or the MANA cryptocurrency.

The platform is built on Ethereum and although largely currently considered a game, the team behind Decentraland have a vision of it becoming a globally used virtual world.

Axie Infinity

Axie Infinity is a game developed by a Vietnamese software company. It is Ethereum-based, where players mint and collect NFTs. In February 2022, the game had generated more than U.S. $4 billion in NFT sales.

The game centers on Axies. These are creatures that players of Axie Infinity collect as pets. Players can breed, raise, and battle their Axies, with the aim being to collect as many as possible. Players can also use the in-game NFTs to purchase a range of other items to expand their collection of Axies and progress through the game. This includes virtual land. In November 2021, a plot of virtual land on Axie Infinity was sold for U.S. $2.3 million.

The game is popular in the Philippines, where players often group together and where some use the game as their main source of income.

Sandbox

Sandbox brings together multiple technologies on a single gaming platform, including blockchain, NFTs, DeFi, and the metaverse. In essence, it is a virtual world where players create or customize a range of different elements, from games within the main game to digital assets such as land, equipment, or fighting behaviors.

Players can then monetize whatever they create by turning them into NFTs and offering them for sale on the in-game marketplace. The cryptocurrencies used to facilitate these transactions is SAND, a cryptocurrency that is native to the game.

As with many other platforms and projects in the metaverse space, Sandbox is Ethereum based and is designed to be used by anyone, including people who don't have technical skills.

Star Atlas

Star Atlas is another game in the metaverse, although this one is set in space and in the future. It is a strategy game, but it doesn't use Ethereum. Instead, it uses the Solana blockchain. In terms of gameplay, however, it is similar to other offerings on the market, as players primarily create, customize, collect, and trade various in-game elements as NFTs.

The goal of the game is to discover new planets as you travel through space, finding the treasures that those planets hold. Players can take on various roles, such as an engineer or aviator, with the gameplay including elements of fighting, crafting, and farming.

One of the things that makes Star Atlas stand out from some other metaverse projects is how realistic the graphics look. One of the ways it achieves this is by using the Unreal Engine.

Key Takeaways

- Blockchain is a particular instantiation of distributed ledger technology. It surfaced with a paper by the entity known as Satoshi Nakamoto in 2008.
- Blockchain bundles transactions together in what is known as a "block." It allows transactions over a trustless network of peers.
- There are many applications of blockchain and more are coming out every day, from decentralized finance to the metaverse.

CHAPTER 6

Blockchain Case Studies

Blockchain technology has a wide range of applications and, as a result, offers benefits in numerous industries (Figure 6.1). Let's look at how blockchain can improve various industries and sectors, including finance, cybersecurity, shipping, and even the metaverse.

Blockchain in Finance

Blockchain technology will eventually completely change financial services as we know them today, bringing about greater efficiency and transparency. One area where blockchain will undoubtedly change things significantly is capital markets.

All those involved in capital markets will benefit from blockchain solutions, including issuers, fund managers, investors, and regulators. Let's look at some of the benefits the different categories of market participants will enjoy.

Issuers

Blockchain will make it easier, faster, and cheaper for issuers to access capital, thanks to programmable digital securities and assets. They will be able to issue new securities in a few minutes, and the associated rights and obligations will be encoded and automated.

Thus, issuers and those who facilitate new issues will be able to accelerate the speed at which they obtain funding, resulting in cheaper and faster growth, along with increased profitability.

Since issuers will be able to program the terms and conditions into the assets they are issuing, these assets will be far more flexible and customizable. Blockchain will also increase transparency and efficiency because investors will be able to access real-time updates via a single interface.

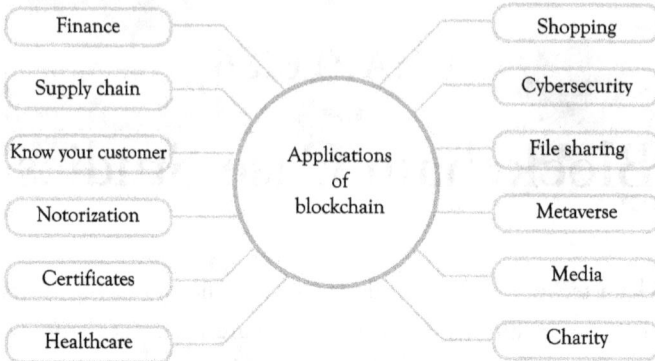

Figure 6.1 Applications of blockchain

Another advantage of blockchain is that issuers will be able to fractionalize each asset. Breaking the asset down into units that are more affordable and easier to transfer means that issuers will be able to enjoy a more diverse investor base and greater liquidity.

The lower barrier to entry also means that smaller issuers will have more opportunities. Furthermore, current issuers will also be able to profit because they'll access new markets and new types of securities.

Fund Managers

At its core, blockchain makes it possible for people to trade assets while ensuring the transaction is registered on a verifiable ledger. In other words, systemic risks and those of defaulting are reduced significantly because funds are more quickly and transparently settled and cleared.

As the transactions will be processed faster, fund managers will have more available capital instead of having it tied up in various transactions. They will, therefore, be able to use and allocate said capital more efficiently.

Funds will also benefit from reduced costs as their operations become more efficient due to simplifying various processes and functions such as accounting, administration, fund servicing, and allocations.

Furthermore, we will likely see a wide range of new financial instruments and products based on blockchain technology. Thus, funds will be able to further diversify their portfolios with novel assets.

Even though many more financial products will be on the market, their structure will be simpler because they will feature specific programmed standards.

Additionally, the ability to issue digital assets and split existing assets into multiple units will provide funds with a broad investor base. This is especially beneficial as younger investors are more likely to invest in digital assets.

Investors

Investors will benefit significantly from blockchain technology because it will provide a level of flexibility no investor has ever seen before. Issuers will be able to issue new securities faster and at a lower cost, which means they'll be able to customize new instruments to the needs and desires of each investor.

As issuers will be able to create investment vehicles that match investors' risk appetite, time horizon, and desire for return, the relationship between investor and issuer will change significantly and become far stronger, creating a bond that hasn't been seen before.

Investors want to make as much money as possible with as little risk as possible. A large contributor to risk is limited liquidity. However, the new financial instruments and digital assets will be programmable and, therefore, carry a lower transaction cost, which will increase their potential liquidity and enable investors to manage their risk better. In conjunction with better connectivity and higher efficiency in capital markets, investors will benefit from a higher degree of liquidity and a lower cost of capital.

The blockchain ledger will also provide investors with better insights into the quality of an asset, making it easier for them to do their due diligence and reducing investment risk.

Regulators

Regulators are often stuck between a rock and a hard place. They're either criticized for getting too involved in capital markets or not acting quickly enough to prevent disasters, as was the case with the 2008 Global Financial Crash.

With blockchain, though, regulatory organizations and agencies will automate a wide range of functions, including compliance and auditing. In addition, since multiple institutions will use the same network to monitor the asset life cycle and their portfolios, regulators will spend more time analyzing and predicting risk instead of trying to figure out the systems each company uses and how they represent their transactions.

Blockchain will also make it possible to minimize any friction that currently arises in labor and time-intensive processes regulators must deal with, thereby streamlining these regulatory and legal processes. Overhead costs will also drop as a result, and it might even be possible to prevent certain types of systemic risk.

A Quick Look at How Blockchain Can Be Used in Capital Markets

Let's look at some use cases of blockchain technology in capital markets.

Issuance

Issuance is the process of creating securities or other investment instruments that are sold to investors to raise capital. Some of the ways blockchains can help include:

- Creating digital representations of existing assets and completely new digital assets.
- Customizing and streamlining securitization of securities and financial instruments.
- Enabling new business models like decentralized crowdfunding to raise capital more efficiently.

Sales and Trading

Sales and trading are essential functions of investment banks and refer to purchasing and selling various financial instruments, including securities. Blockchain makes it easier to bring digital securities to market by employing various mechanisms, including:

- Bilateral negotiations
- Centralized exchanges
- Decentralized exchanges
- Matching algorithms
- Auctions

Blockchain offers a wide range of new opportunities, including creating new digital financial instruments tailored to investor needs.

Collateral Management

The current processes used for collateral management are highly inefficient and slow due to the need for manual reconciliation and the physical delivery of the financial instruments. This limits the ability to react to quickly changing market conditions.

There's also the problem of siloed information, making it virtually impossible to get a high-level overview of collateral assets.

Blockchain streamlines collateral management processes by digitizing the holdings and registering them in a single and optimized location. Furthermore, smart contracts can improve precision by automating margin calls while invoking preset rules for every relationship.

Exchanges

Blockchain can streamline exchange operations for a wide range of the functions they perform. This technology will help reduce trading fees while also ensuring quicker clearing and settlement, leading to lower overheads and improved processes.

The transparent ledger can also help exchanges when it comes to verifying data and access rights. Furthermore, it could even act as a robust warning system regarding trading activity.

Clearing and Settlement

Clearing refers to updating accounts and preparing to transfer securities and money, while settlement refers to actually completing the exchange.

Entities can program smart contracts to match transfers and payments via off-chain cash payments, stablecoins, or cryptocurrencies. In terms of settlement, a variety of models can be used for matching that consider the market's liquidity needs as well as risk tolerance. Such models include deferred settlement, atomic settlement, and deferred net settlement.

Blockchain Applications in Supply Chains

Supply chains have become increasingly complex and, in many cases, global, which means that their management involves various demanding processes. Moreover, all these processes need to be perfectly orchestrated and synchronized as they involve numerous actors and have many moving parts.

As a result, the connections required to distribute goods and services have evolved from a chain to resemble a web. The problem is that when these processes grow to include multiple stages and a wide range of agents spanning numerous countries, transparency tends to decline. As more people become part of the process, complexity increases, as do the challenges.

Blockchain technology can benefit all the main parts that an active supply chain consists of, namely:

- Development sourcing
- Production logistics
- Information systems management
- Coordination

Supply chain management also includes other essential fields, such as logistics, shipping, freight, trucking, and other cargo transport forms. And blockchain can benefit any area where systems need to be streamlined in multiple ways.

Companies can significantly improve overly complex and sluggish supply chains, thanks to blockchain. The end-to-end decentralized processes offered by blockchain-based supply chain solutions have led to industries changing the way they do business.

Massive companies such as IBM have become aware of what blockchain can do for managing supply chains and, as a result, have already started work on solutions to help.

In some cases, the technology has already been implemented. As a result, experts feel that blockchain stands a good chance of becoming a "universal operating system" for supply chain management, a bit like Windows or iOS for PCs and Macs, respectively.

Blockchain could streamline such tasks as:

- Registering the quantity of assets and their transfer as they move between the different points in the supply chain.
- Tracking all trade-related documents, including purchase and change orders, receipts, and shipment notifications.
- Assigning or validating the properties or certifications of various products, such as establishing whether food is fair trade or organic.
- Associating serial numbers, digital tags, bar codes, and the like to physical goods.
- Providing suppliers and vendors with all the information they need regarding manufacturing processes, assembly, delivery, and product maintenance.

Thanks to blockchain, companies involved in the supply chain will enjoy benefits such as:

- Improved transparency as the product's journey throughout the supply chain will be documented every step of the way, thereby revealing the real origin. This will help improve trust and reduce the current bias that supply chains suffer from.
- Increased scalability because it is possible to have almost any number of users accessing the network from an unlimited number of touchpoints.
- Improved security, thanks to a shared ledger that cannot be modified unilaterally and features codified rules, which could result in the reduction or elimination of process and system audits.

Introducing TradeLens From Maersk and IBM

Maersk and IBM teamed up and created TradeLens, which is a block-chain-based shipping solution ("TradeLens | Digitizing Global Supply Chains" n.d.). The goal is to improve the efficiency and security of global trade while encouraging innovation in the industry by bringing parties together to support sharing of information and improving transparency.

As of this writing, the two companies had already announced that 94 organizations were actively involved or had agreed to participate in the open-standard platform. Thus, the TradeLens platform already included many participants, including port and terminal operators, global container carriers, customs authorities, cargo owners, and more.

Relying on IBM blockchain technology, TradeLens helps improve collaboration between multiple trading partners by ensuring everyone has access to a single, shared view of a particular transaction without giving away private and confidential information.

As a result, shippers, shipping companies, freight forwarders, port and terminal operators, inland transport firms, and customs authorities can improve the efficiency of their interactions because they have access to shipping data and documents in real time, including sensor and IoT information.

Thanks to smart contracts, TradeLens makes it possible for the different parties involved in international trade to collaborate easily and effectively.

The platform also comes with a trade document module named ClearWay. This module allows the collaboration of importers/exporters, customs brokers, customs authorities, other government agencies, and NGOs in various processes and information sharing. As expected with blockchain, all these collaborations are supported by a secure audit trail that can't be challenged.

The TradeLens platform will reduce obstacles impeding global trade while also making international supply chains more efficient. It will make a containerized shipping trade platform available, which means that the whole supply chain environment will be connected.

Supported by blockchain technology and developed on an open technology stack, the platform will deal with issues such as lack of visibility and documentation problems.

Essentially, it ensures that all the parties involved in a global shipping transaction will be able to see the entire supply chain from start to finish and easily and securely access data pertinent to these transactions in real time.

It will also improve efficiencies, thanks to the digitization and automation of paperwork. End users will be able to securely submit, stamp, and approve documents beyond organizational and national borders.

Blockchain in KYC, Notarization, and Certificates

Blockchain and distributed ledger technology will also eliminate the likelihood of fraudulent activity or errors regarding the authenticity of legal documentation and its content. Certificates and other legal documents can be issued and verified on a public or private ledger, providing a verifiable trail.

Currently, most industries verify this information manually via paper documents. Unfortunately, this is a time-intensive and resource-heavy process.

So, how would this work with blockchain?

First, the signature or fingerprint of the document would have to be issued on the blockchain. This would mean converting the records into a digital file, such as a pdf that one could also attach metadata to.

Subsequently, the digital document's data would be used, and special algorithms would be applied to create a unique signature. Hash functions (special mathematical functions) are usually used to derive these signatures. They act as a unique identifier, akin to a bar or QR code, but only applicable to that document.

The signature is then registered on the blockchain by connecting the signature to an action or transaction on the ledger.

Of course, if one takes advantage of decentralized storage systems like IPFS, the complete certificate can be uploaded, providing another layer of authentication.

Next, the content can be verified using blockchain technology.

This means determining the document's unique signature via the algorithm the issuer used to create the signature. Then, one would use the issuer's application to search for the signature on the blockchain. If the two signatures match, the certificate is valid.

DNV: A Case Study

Many companies are attempting to create solutions that will automate issuing and verifying paper documents ("DNV.Com—When Trust Matters" n.d.). DNV relies on a blockchain-based solution that relies on QR code technology to issue and validate supply-chain certificates.

With DNV, the certificates are stored on a private or permissioned blockchain network. This means that only DNV (the issuers) can create new certificates or change the data. They can also take advantage of the technology's other benefits, such as decentralization, encryption, and authentication.

While only DNV can update the data, everyone has access to the blockchain to verify and authenticate certificates.

How Does It Work?

When the company issues a certificate, they digitize the data, and each certificate is assigned a digital identity. As such, all certificates are traceable and have been tagged, with the original stored safely on the nodes that make up the blockchain.

In parallel, the data the certificate contains is managed in the company's production system. The end result is an immutable transaction that is secure and transparent. This makes it easy to discover fraud because the blockchain will quickly show if any certificates are outdated or forgeries.

To check authenticity, all certificates feature embedded QR codes that can be scanned by any device that has a QR scanner. A search is conducted on the blockchain, and the certificate details will be shown. Thus, anyone can check the claims of a company and the validity of the certificate.

DNV also has a public certificate checker that can be used to check the validity of a certificate.

Hanseaticsoft: Another Case Study

Hanseaticsoft is a consortium that is developing a seafarer certification system based on blockchain technology ("Cloud Fleet Manager by Hanseaticsoft" n.d.). The goal is to streamline and speed up various processes encumbered by current certificate management systems that are all paper-based, the absence of safety document verification, and no access to validate the training and safety certification of seafarers.

All the aforementioned can cause many problems for ship operators, regulatory and port authorities, and crew management agencies in securing and insuring crew members.

The consortium has brought together a wide array of stakeholders who support or rely on crew certification, including shipping companies such as Maersk, Heidmar, and PTC Holdings Crop.

Other tech enablers with certification expertise are also involved, such as providers of maritime platforms like Navozyme and C-LOG.

The project will focus on demonstrating the effectiveness of using a digital certification and endorsement process that will rely on a digital repository to store and authenticate verified documentation and training logs and an approval system.

Essentially, the system would allow individual seafarers to manage certificates when they are originally issued. It will also make it easier for maritime administrations to manage cross-jurisdiction renewal and endorsement. At the same time, crew management firms will be better able to keep track of seafarers to crew vessels. Finally, ship owners will be able to access an overview of their crew, along with their certifications and endorsements.

Blockchain in Shipping

While we discussed how blockchain could improve supply chains earlier, let's look more closely at how it can help the shipping industry.

IoT and Blockchain in the Shipping Industry

IoT refers to everyday objects that can connect to each other and beyond using the Internet, which allows them to send and receive data. For example, think of a smart refrigerator that can connect to the Internet and order groceries you are low on.

IoT is quite prevalent in shipping because companies deploy sensors on ships, cargo, and containers to track their status for a variety of data processing purposes such as optimizing fuel consumption, improving craft and cargo data management, improving predictive maintenance, reducing emissions, and much more.

Adding blockchain to the IoT mix provides a verifiable, permanent, and secure way of recording the data these smart devices process. The blockchain guarantees that all the data in the ledger has been verified by the network's peers and fulfilled all the necessary conditions.

The quality of the data is essential when it comes to data analytics. As the saying goes, garbage in, garbage out, regardless of how advanced and sophisticated the algorithms to analyze the data are.

A blockchain-based network of these interconnected devices will be able to interact with the world around them and make decisions without the need for human involvement, which will increase efficiency, lower costs, and, as a result, improve overheads.

Digitizing Paper-Based Processes

Despite being in the so-called digital age, shipping transactions still involve ridiculous amounts of paperwork, from sales contracts and charter party agreements to bills of lading and letter of credit. The list is endless.

While all this paperwork is a necessary evil, the problem is that it results in cumbersome operations because many of the stakeholders involved rely on the generation, authorization, and distribution of a large volume of paper documents. All these documents must be passed along a chain of numerous parties, with each having to take some form of action, such as initiation of payment, collection and delivery of cargo, and so on.

With blockchain technology, all these paper-based operations could be eliminated. All the actors involved in the transaction could rely on blockchain and smart contract technology to remain in contact, carry out physical transactions, store and share encrypted information, carry out their contractual obligations, issue and receive instructions, and make secure payments.

Traceability of Valuable Items

Combining blockchain and tagging technology means that products can be tracked throughout the supply chain, from their origin to their final destination. Not only will this increase consumer trust, but it will also make it easier to achieve law and standard compliance.

Some would argue that tracing products throughout their journey is one of the most powerful and logical applications of blockchain technology.

With blockchain, there is only truth. Everyone has access to immutable records that track items from creation to distribution, which can be extremely beneficial for high-value products such as electronics, designer goods, pharmaceuticals, and more.

Reducing and Authenticating Counterfeit Products

Blockchain's transparency will streamline processes in the shipping world by allowing companies to monitor cargo capacity in real time, thereby addressing potential supply chain bottlenecks before they occur.

However, it's also a technology that might help with the problem of counterfeiting, which is becoming more and more prevalent. Not only does counterfeiting cost companies billions of dollars every year, but it also damages their brands.

Blockchain will make it much harder for counterfeit goods to enter the supply chain by allowing the traceability of goods from their origin to the end user.

Raising Capital Through Tokenization

Tokenization can be used to finance shipping companies, providing the industry with a greater level of liquidity. However, it should be noted that tokenization in the shipping industry will require an effective regulatory and legal framework in the country where it will launch.

A Look at Some Blockchain Applications in the Shipping and Logistics Sector

In this section, we'll take a quick look at some of the applications that have been or are being developed for the shipping and logistics industry.

ShipChain

ShipChain with the associated SHIP token is a project that intends to create a completely integrated system from one end of the supply chain to the other. Therefore, it will cover everything from the moment the cargo leaves the manufacturer to when it reaches the customer. It is supported by transparent blockchain contracts and is federated in trustless.

At first, this product will mainly focus on container ships and will attempt to develop:

- End-to-end tracking and tracing to replace the current poor systems.
- Rewards for transporting efficiently to improve responsibility.
- Increased transparency by enabling direct contact between charterers and carriers.
- Better visibility as all documentation will be available on the blockchain network.

CargoX

CargoX, with the associated COX token, intends to be an independent supplier of blockchain-based bills of lading (B/Ls). These B/Ls will completely change the face of international trade and shipping because, rather than waiting for days or weeks for the B/L to go through the banks to get to the receiver, everyone will be able to access them using a specific cryptographic key.

It will also help reduce fraud, improve safety, lower costs, and increase reliability.

IMMLA

IMMLA, with the associated IML token, is an Ethereum-based logistics app focused on multimodal transportation. The goal is to allow carriers and cargo owners to interact directly at every stage of the multimodal transport chain.

Essentially, IMMLA will act as a freight manager using the entire carriage chain. As you might expect, cargo owners will be able to benefit from multimodal transport that's far more efficient and cost-effective, thanks to this platform.

iXledger

iXledger and its associated IXT token is not a dedicated shipping app. Instead, it's the first blockchain-supported marketplace to trade and manage insurance products, including marine insurance.

With this marketplace, shipping companies will have a lot more options not only in terms of insurance but also quicker access to the policies they need. IXT tokens will be the currency used to cover the cost of both the insurance services and transaction fees on the platform.

Shipowner.io

Shipowner.io, with the associated SHIP token, intends to be the first blockchain-supported platform that will provide the shipping industry with options to finance assets. The goal is to break up the current consolidation of financiers by giving shipping companies access to a greater pool of potential investors.

The SHIP token will provide access to the platform, and people will be able to invest as little as a few dollars in a ship, though it will all be done transparently. In essence, it is a form of crowdfunding for ships.

Fr8

Fr8, with its associated Fr8 token, uses smart contracts to enable carriers and shippers the easy coordination of freight. This marketplace aims to reduce the level of inefficiency in the freight market, namely the fact that demand seems to exceed supply, yet there are a lot of empty trucks traveling the roads.

The Fr8 platform also claims that it makes tracking easier and more efficient. It can also provide proof of delivery that's recorded in a blockchain network and can't be altered and offer settlement services, thereby reducing the carrier's credit risk.

Blockchain in Cybersecurity

Probably the most well-known blockchain-based application globally, the Bitcoin network is made up of thousands (if not tens of thousands) of computers known as nodes. Individuals or groups operate these computers across the world. This decentralized network based on blockchain is immutable, meaning that the data transactions cannot be reversed.

Blockchain's decentralization makes it perfect for cybersecurity. It ensures the integrity of the data, automates the storage, and offers complete transparency. So let's explore how blockchain can help with cybersecurity.

Cybersecurity: A Snapshot of Now and the Future

Every day, the amount of data we generate increases by leaps and bounds. As technology progresses and becomes more sophisticated, especially in terms of security, bad actors are coming up with new approaches and robust technology to carry out their nefarious activities.

This has led to some frightening cybersecurity statistics. For example, 95 percent of data breaches are the result of human error. In the first six months of 2020 alone, over 35 billion records were exposed by data breaches. Of these, 45 percent were the result of hacking, 22 percent of phishing, while 17 percent were caused by malware (IBM 2021).

Overall, cybercrime caused damages of approximately $6 trillion in 2021, with ransomware alone costing businesses more than $75 billion per year.

Clearly, the situation is escalating and will continue to get worse. As 5G networks expand, download speeds will spike, which will only give hackers more opportunities to discover security problems. The ability to download faster will also result in even greater cybercrimes.

The increased appetite for IoT on a commercial level means that companies are developing all sorts of applications, including devices for smart homes. Unfortunately, this means that bad actors can take advantage of inefficient security features, where blockchain technology can help.

Furthermore, people are turning to an increasing number of social media platforms to connect with others worldwide. The passwords used to protect these accounts are often weak, which means hackers can access the huge quantity of metadata generated by social media activity.

Blockchain technology can help by developing standard security protocols because it's more effective than end-to-end encryption. It can also boost private messaging security by creating a unified API framework that will allow people to communicate across various messenger apps.

With less-than-stellar security features, edge devices, such as smart switches, have allowed hackers to get into smart homes and other systems. Blockchain technology can secure both individual devices and overall systems by ensuring their administration is decentralized.

Decentralizing things like Domain Name System (DNS) entries means that blockchain can be used to avert Distributed Denial of Service (DDoS) attacks.

The problem is that if we keep centralizing stored data, the risk of exposure increases because all it takes is one vulnerability that a hacker can exploit.

Conversely, taking a decentralized approach via blockchain technology will make it unfeasible for bad actors to penetrate data storage systems.

Blockchain technology can also be used to validate and verify activities such as patching, installations, and updating firmware. It can also protect against unauthorized access of data during transit through encryption.

Blockchain and File Sharing

Decentralized file sharing represents a file storage method that employs multiple network nodes instead of a single central server.

The centralized approach to file sharing is problematic because the Internet has grown into a massive and complicated web of files and information that connect via the Hypertext Transfer Protocol (HTTP). The increase in Internet traffic means that the amount of data now being transmitted is colossal, and the currently used protocol is not dealing with it well.

For example, every time you visit your favorite news site and load a page, your computer uses HTTP to get the content from a centralized server. However, if the server needs to send over a massive file, it could use up a lot of bandwidth.

Furthermore, if the server goes offline for whatever reason, the website might be there, but some things could be missing. It also makes it easier to censor information when all the data is stored in a central location.

One solution that has appeared is decentralized file sharing. One example of this approach that you might be familiar with is torrenting, which is a way to distribute very large files via the Internet without using HTTP.

However, the existing solutions aren't perfect because volunteers generally operate the nodes. In other words, they do it for free and when they can. And they can stop operating the note whenever they like, meaning that there is little guarantee there will be sufficient nodes to host all these files.

Blockchain technology could help create a robust file-sharing network where people have a reason to keep their node active because they'll be rewarded for it. Implementing a reward scheme that offers tokens will ensure that the network has sufficient nodes to keep running.

How Does It Work?

When you get your files from a centralized server, you are using a client–server model. In other words, you are the client, and you ask for what you want by typing in the URL, which points to an IP address based on where the server is that's storing the data. The server then uses HTTP to deliver what you asked for.

Conversely, with a decentralized file-sharing system, you'll be using a peer-to-peer (P2P) sharing system. In this case, files aren't stored just on one server. Instead, they are stored on multiple nodes in the network. In addition, each file or file fragment has a unique cryptographic hash, which means that all versions of the file are tracked across the network.

When the user asks for the data in question, the network will locate the nodes that have the files with that unique hash and then deliver the files.

What Are the Advantages of Decentralized File Sharing?

With blockchain, the files are distributed across multiple computers. When combined with hash addresses, the content will always be available, but it is unchangeable. In other words, even if one computer drops out of the equation, it won't interrupt service because the other nodes will take over and deliver a duplicate of the file.

When you access data from a centralized server via HTTP, the service tends to be a bit slower. Conversely, far less bandwidth will be used with the decentralized approach because the files are distributed across multiple channels.

With blockchain, censorship is also far less likely. Normally, a government can demand that the Internet service providers in a country block access to a service or website by refusing access to that particular IP address. However, when the data of a website is stored on multiple nodes across a network, one cannot block it.

Blockchain and the Metaverse

The metaverse is coming. Some say it will be here in 10 years; others believe it will be far sooner. And blockchain will be able to significantly improve many of the associated projects.

But what is the metaverse?

Essentially, the metaverse is a virtual environment consisting of different worlds allowing you to access a variety of apps and services. These would be individual spaces based on application and use case.

What's interesting to note is that many people don't think the metaverse has a future. However, its quick progress proves that these opinions might not be warranted. New projects are springing up every day and connecting with one another to create bridges between all the aspects of people's online lives.

However, blockchain will be crucial to the continued successful development of the metaverse. But how?

Well, at the moment, most of the projects being developed for the metaverse are essentially games that provide the 3D view of this new virtual ecosystem. However, we'll need many more components to truly build a robust environment that will work as intended.

Blockchain (or crypto) will help expand on functionalities, thereby assisting the metaverse in becoming everything it can be. Here are some ways that can happen:

Proof of Ownership

With blockchain, providing proof that you own assets in the metaverse will no longer be a problem. You can have a crypto wallet, and the associated private keys can prove that you own specific assets or activities. Therefore, a crypto project in the metaverse could have a strong and very secure methodology of proving ownership and verifying your digital identity.

Value Transfer

Another critical aspect to making the metaverse successful is the ability to conduct a value transfer. In other words, if you want to sell something, you have to be able to transfer the "object" and receive payment, which also represents a transfer.

So, people will need a safe and trusted way to transfer value. For example, crypto is a safer alternative than a multiplayer game's currency on the blockchain. Therefore, crypto could be a good currency for people who want to spend a long time in the metaverse.

Interoperability

A key aspect when it comes to the feasibility of projects in the metaverse is interoperability, which blockchain can facilitate. This technology can ensure that the metaverse's different worlds and spaces are compatible with each other and work seamlessly.

For example, projects such as Polkadot and Avalanche allow you to develop custom blockchain networks that can work with each other.

Governance

The metaverse is meant to be a virtual representation of the real world, which means we will need rules. However, thanks to blockchain, we can have fair and transparent governance in the metaverse, which is not something we see in the real world.

Establishing Uniqueness of Collectible Items

Another essential aspect of metaverse projects is digital collection. For an item to be collectible, it must be unique and original, which means you must prove that the asset you own meets these criteria. Blockchain technology makes it easy to provide proof via NFTs, which means completely unique assets can be created.

Furthermore, blockchain technology can be used to create digital representations of physical assets to, once again, provide proof of ownership, originality, and uniqueness.

Examples of Metaverse Projects

Let's take a quick look at some metaverse projects.

Decentraland

Decentraland can be called a 3D universe where players can build up plots of digital real estate. They can participate in a whole range of activities, including hosting events, engaging in other social endeavors, and creating content.

This simple 2D game has become a highly popular project, with NFTs valued in the hundreds of thousands of dollars.

Bloktopia

Another interesting project is Bloktopia, which is essentially a virtual reality game where one joins an environment that mimics a skyscraper. With 21 floors representing the maximum Bitcoin supply, the project means to provide people with a place to socialize, work, hold events, and engage in a variety of other activities in the metaverse.

Blockchain enables four main functionalities in Bloktopia: earning, creating, playing, and learning. It has its own native token (BLOK).

Bloktopia also allows advertising via Adblok and facilitates real estate via Reblok. Users can also create their games or play games other users have created.

Sandbox

The Sandbox is a blockchain game that allows people to discover a virtual world. It includes NFTs, environments created by users, and all sorts of other content.

This project has grown into a complex environment that relies on Ether and its native token (SAND) to run the game's economy.

Players have the option of creating a digital avatar and identity to which they can connect a crypto wallet to manage their SAND tokens, NFTs, and other assets. Players can also create virtual items and games.

NFT Projects

Bored Ape Yacht Club

Bored Ape Yacht Club is a collection of NFTs made up of cartoon apes created by an algorithm that used 170 different traits, from expressions to clothing to added items. There are 10,000 of these cartoon apes in the collection. It is a project built on the Ethereum blockchain, so Ether is used to purchase Bored Ape NFTs.

Bored Ape Yacht Club is owned by Yuga labs and launched in 2021. Buying and owning a Bored Ape NFT gives you intellectual property rights over the image. In other words, you become the owner of the original cartoon ape artwork. This ownership is recorded on the blockchain. Ownership of a Bored Ape NFT means you also become a member of a private online club.

Sales since its launch are in excess of U.S. $1 billion. In fact, Bored Ape Yacht Club is an NFT project that has set new standards, becoming the highest priced NFTs on the market and leading the NFT sales charts for much of the first quarter of 2022.

The average purchase price of a Bored Ape NFT is hundreds of thousands of dollars, with many of them owned by celebrities. Snoop Dogg, Eminem, Paris Hilton, Serena Williams, and Jimmy Fallon are among the Bored Ape NFT celebrity owners. The company Adidas also owns a Bored Ape NFT.

The price for a Bored Ape NFT varies, often depending on how rare it is. For example, there are only 26 Bored Ape NFTs where the cartoon ape is depicted with a slice of pizza hanging out of its mouth.

It hasn't all been smooth sailing for the Bored Ape Yacht Club, though. The designs have come in for criticism in some quarters, and it has suffered cyberattacks, including a hack on its Discord chat channel.

Despite the challenges, all 10,000 Bored Ape NFTs sold out. They are now traded on OpenSea, the NFT marketplace.

The success of the Bored Ape Yacht is often put down to the fact that owners of Bored Ape NFTs can use the image however they want, including to make money or as a digital identity. The high price tags for Bored Ape NFTs also make them a status symbol, increasing their appeal.

Cryptopunks

Cryptopunks is an NFT project that is similar to the Bored Ape Yacht Club, as it is also a collection of NFTs built on the Ethereum block-chain. It predates Bored Ape, however, as it was launched in 2017. It was launched by Larva Labs, but Cryptopunks is now owned by Yuga Labs, the people behind Bored Ape Yacht Club.

The concept of Cryptopunks is based on the punk scene in London, with further inspiration taken from music from artists like Daft Punk. There are 10,000 Cryptopunks in the collection, about two-thirds of which are male and the rest female. Like Bored Ape NFTs, Cryptopunks NFTs were created by an algorithm. Those Cryptopunks with the rarest character traits are typically the most valuable. There are different character types, as well, with the rarest usually claiming the biggest price tags.

Cryptopunks is widely recognized as having sparked widespread interest in NFTs, although the original Cryptopunks NFTs were essentially given away for free. Today, they are most commonly traded on the NFT marketplace OpenSea. They don't sell for as much as Bored Ape NFTs, but they are still in a six-figure price range.

Total sales of Cryptopunks NFTs are now over U.S. $2 billion, with some being sold at mainstream auction houses like Christies.

There are a few reasons why Cryptopunks NFTs have been popular and continue to be sought after. The fact that they are one of the oldest NFT projects is a key consideration. They were also the first to use algorithmically created images, and approach now copied by many other NFT projects, including Bored Ape Yacht Club.

The fact that each Cryptopunks NFT is unique is also a factor in their popularity. Like Bored Ape NFTs, they are used online as digital identities. When Yuga Labs acquired the Cryptopunks intellectual property, it granted all Cryptopunks owners full commercial rights over their NFTs.

Key Takeaways

- There are many applications of blockchain in different fields. In this chapter, we covered finance, shipping, cybersecurity, file sharing, and the metaverse.
- Blockchains applications usually help with issues of trust, or unnecessary friction.
- In the metaverse, blockchain has become a prominent characteristic primarily through the use of NFT ownership and new monetization avenues.
- Two of the most popular NFT projects are the Bored Ape Yacht Club and Cryptopunks. Many more are definitely going to appear in the future.

CHAPTER 7

Where Do You Stand Now on the Maturity Curve?

The maturity curve is a way to think about the level of adoption for a certain technology. There are different stages in this curve, each more mature than the previous one. The initial stage, called Innovation Trigger, is where innovative companies experiment with new technologies.

When they see that there is some competitive advantage in using it, they start investing more in it and move to the next stage—Early Adopter—when they start using it on a larger scale. However, it's not until later that you will see the full adoption of the technology by most companies—Late Majority—when it has become mainstream.

Emerging technologies present unique opportunities and challenges, as many organizations find it challenging to adopt disruptive technologies due to their revolutionary nature, which often requires a change in mindset.

This final chapter will provide some frameworks to assess your organization's capabilities and the industry's potential to be disrupted by AI and blockchain.

Assessing AI/Data Science Capabilities

We propose a framework to assist organizations in evaluating their AI and data science capabilities.

The framework has been developed from a series of workshops with senior executives from across a number of industries. We address the need for a common language to discuss AI and data science capabilities and how they can be assessed. The framework provides a common understanding of the terminology and a set of key indicators for measuring current and potential AI and data science capabilities.

AI Maturity

The concept of AI maturity related to a company refers to the different levels of adoption and determines how much value that business can derive from AI solutions. To achieve full adoption, however, companies must tackle four key components:

1. Knowledge
2. Data
3. Culture
4. Talent

Let's look more closely at each of these.

Knowledge

Knowledge has two subcomponents, namely conceptual understanding and the AI bible. In terms of conceptual understanding, key stakeholders must know how AI works, including basic AI terms and components and an idea of representative use-cases.

This doesn't mean that management suddenly needs to learn to code. However, they must have an understanding of why their business' data is valuable and why the format is just as vital. They also need to learn how algorithms leverage data and what sorts of results can be obtained from such algorithms.

In terms of representative use-cases, it's essential for key stakeholders to understand what others in their industry are doing with AI (and why they're succeeding.) So, for example, a business in the e-commerce space should be aware of how Amazon is leveraging AI to boost their business.

The AI bible component refers to internal knowledge in the sense that businesses need to create a foundation of knowledge to achieve full AI adoption. This includes frameworks for maintaining existing AI projects and deploying new AI systems.

Data

When it comes to data, two overarching elements are vital: data access and quality and data value.

Companies should be prepared to run pilot data science projects to determine what works best for their situation. Without hands-on experience and experimentation, a company will waste time and resources without any valuable insights to show for it.

Experimentation is also essential because it can provide companies with the insights needed to improve data quality.

Furthermore, businesses must improve data accessibility. Unfortunately, many companies still run using old models where data is often siloed by department (or even more granular), which completely derails any chance of turning data into something usable. Therefore, improving accessibility so that everyone who needs access to the data can quickly find what they need is essential.

Data governance policies are one essential way to achieve this improved level of accessibility.

In terms of data value, companies need to develop ways to maintain, store, and access the data they already have. Protocols should be implemented to detail clear instructions regarding how to handle and maintain existing data assets.

Furthermore, data only really has value if it's being used consistently. In other words, businesses need to be using their data all the time. Otherwise, they'll never be able to determine what is valuable and what isn't.

Culture

The fact is that AI adoption often lags due to culture. People in the "know" might be all gung-ho about adopting something new, but many aren't that knowledgeable and are often worried about change.

Even when adoption occurs, the results aren't the best because crucial parties are still on the fence and don't understand what's going on.

Therefore, it's critical that all stakeholders understand what benefits can be derived from AI and how to gain those benefits. And it all starts with a willingness to experiment and iterate.

It means understanding that it won't be perfect from the start, which is why iteration is necessary. With every iteration, the result will improve significantly. However, expecting miracles out of the gate is a recipe for disaster because when those expectations aren't met, stakeholders might start pointing fingers.

Experimentation is just as critical as iteration. After all, if you don't try anything, you'll have difficulty figuring out what works. And with how quickly AI is advancing practically every day, there is always something new to try that might deliver far better results than expected.

It's also essential to learn the value of cross-functional collaboration. An AI project will only be successful if the key stakeholders and teams collaborate. Therefore, it's vital for companies to remove silos and promote communication and collaboration between departments.

Talent

Talent is one of the most important aspects. Without the right talent, companies won't be able to achieve the best possible results. In fact, without the right team with a good leader, a business is far more likely to fail than succeed, which is why getting the right people on board is so critical.

Where Is Your Business?

Based on the statements that follow, determine your business AI maturity level, which will help you determine what you need to work on to get closer to your goal of full AI adoption.

Knowledge

1. No knowledge of AI or data science.
2. The organization has some understanding, but this is limited to its technical team.
3. The middle management has an understanding of how data science/ AI could be applied to its respective function.
4. The c-suite has a strategic understanding of AI, and it has a data strategy, perhaps even hiring someone at the c-level to oversee it.

Data

1. The organization is simply collecting data.
2. The organization is utilizing data.
3. The organization has data quality checks in place.
4. The organization has some ideas about data products or has created some data products, including products for internal use (e.g., dashboards) or external use (customer-facing).

Data-Driven Culture

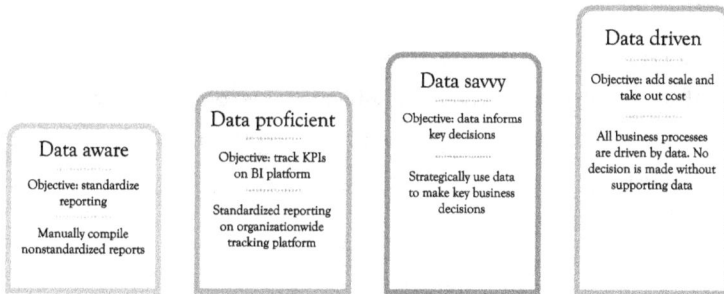

Figure 7.1 Stages of a data-driven culture

Talent

Table 7.1 Skill gap analysis to determine talent needs

Analysis	1 Existing Resource	2 Existing (Retrain)	3 New Hire	4 Consultant	5 Service Provider/ Partner	Summary
Data Governance						
Data Quality						
Data Architecture						
Developer						
Data Infrastructure/Engineer						
Analyst and BI (business intelligence)						
Change/Technical Project Managers						

Assessing Blockchain Capabilities and Potential

In this section, we present a framework that can help an organization understand whether blockchain can be applied to a particular problem.

After you answer these questions, you'll have a better idea of whether blockchain is suited for your business or not. You'll also know if blockchain is the best solution for the problem you're tackling. Essentially, this framework is meant to help you figure out if blockchain will help your business and what type of solution you're looking for.

Business

1. What problem do you need to solve?
2. If the problem doesn't require solving at least one issue related to the following, blockchain might not be the right option.
   a. Costs
   b. Efficiency
   c. Redundancy
   d. Trust
   e. Transparency
   f. Security
   g. Censorship
3. What sort of coordination is necessary?
   a. Is it an internal or external solution?
   b. If it's external, is the ecosystem developed enough in terms of:
      i. Developers
      ii. Academia
      iii. Industry bodies
      iv. Customers
      v. Corporates and institutions
      vi. Entrepreneurs and small and medium businesses
      vii. Investors
      viii. Suppliers
4. Is it a B2C or B2B problem? B2C issues will be subject to more demanding regulatory requirements, and creating the right ecosystem will also be more challenging.

5. How complex and novel is the solution?
   a. Is it a solution that requires a low level of novelty and coordination, making it less expensive and more highly focused?
   b. Does the solution consist of high-novelty innovations requiring fewer users to generate value right away?
   c. Is it a solution that comprises low-novelty innovation but a high degree of coordination with outside stakeholders?
   d. Is the solution one where a lot of innovation and coordination is necessary, making it a transformative solution?

Technology

1. What type of blockchain would be best suited for the solution you've developed?
2. Is the ecosystem for your distributed ledger technology sufficiently developed, that is, do you already have a DApp for your solution?
3. What other solution could you use other than blockchain? In other words, would a relational database achieve the same thing?

Legal

1. Is your solution so innovative that there's no regulatory precedent?
2. If rules and legislation exist, how friendly is the jurisdiction?
   a. In terms of where your company will be located?
   b. In terms of where your customers are located?
3. Do you have access to any financial and legal guidance?
   a. Can you get help through existing regulations?
   b. Do you have any AML (Anti-Money Laundering) or KYC (Know Your Customer) issues to tackle, and can you get help?
4. Do you have to consider any other directives and regulations, such as GDPR?
   a. Do you have access to assistance regarding privacy and digital identity issues?
5. Does your solution seem fair to everyone within the ecosystem, especially customers?
6. How reliable are the oracles you're using?

7. How will your solution affect competing companies in the ecosystem?

8. Will your solution create and encourage trust in the ecosystem?

Summary

Emerging technologies are here to stay. And the organizations that are ready for them will have a competitive edge. We can prepare for the future by being mindful of changes in the environment, adapting to the changing landscape, and understanding how these emerging technologies are likely to impact our strategy.

The first step is to be mindful of the changes in the environment that are happening now. The second is adapting to these changes and adjusting your business strategy accordingly. The third is forecasting new technologies that will impact your business strategy.

One of the most challenging aspects of building a successful organization is understanding what the future has in store for us. To be successful in the future, any organization needs to prepare itself for change by anticipating how it will evolve to meet these changes.

The future is not only possible but it's also inevitable. We hope that this book has helped you see the emerging technologies that will dominate the near future in a different light and will assist you in navigating this competitive landscape.

Bibliography

Allen, F.E. 2001. "The Myth of Artificial Intelligence." *American Heritage* www
.americanheritage.com/myth-artificial-intelligence

"Artificial Intelligence Has a Problem With Gender and Racial Bias." n.d. *Time*.
https://time.com/5520558/artificial-intelligence-racial-gender-bias/ (accessed
January 27, 2022).

Barba, P. September 29, 2020. "Machine Learning (ML) for Natural Language
Processing(NLP)." *Lexalytics*. www.lexalytics.com/lexablog/machine-learning-
natural-language-processing

Beyer, S. August 23, 2018. "Blockchain Before Bitcoin: A History." *Block Telegraph*
(blog). https://blocktelegraph.io/blockchain-before-bitcoin-history/

Buchanan, B.G., and E.H. Shortliffe, eds. 1984. "Rule-Based Expert Systems:
The MYCIN Experiments of the Stanford Heuristic Programming Project."
The Addison-Wesley Series in Artificial Intelligence. Reading, Mass: Addison-
Wesley.

"Check Your Symptoms | Medicare." n.d. *Medicare.Gov*. www.medicare.gov/
manage-your-health/share-your-medicare-claims-medicares-blue-button/
check-your-symptoms (accessed January 27, 2022).

"Cloud Fleet Manager by Hanseaticsoft." n.d. https://hanseaticsoft.com/ (accessed
January 27, 2022).

Conway, F., and J. Siegelman. 2005. *Dark Hero of the Information Age: In Search
of Norbert Wiener, the Father of Cybernetics*. New York, NY: Basic Books.

Crevier, D. 1993. *AI: The Tumultuous History of the Search for Artificial Intelligence*.
New York, NY: Basic Books.

Dilip, D. n.d. "Application of Statistics in Business." RVS Institute of Management
Studies and Research. www.rvsimsr.ac.in/blog/application-statistics-business
.php (accessed January 27, 2022).

"DNV.Com—When Trust Matters." n.d. *DNV*. www.dnv.com/Default (accessed
January 27, 2022).

"European Data Strategy." n.d. Text. European Commission—European
Commission. https://ec.europa.eu/info/strategy/priorities-2019-2024/europe
-fit-digital-age/european-data-strategy_en (accessed January 27, 2022).

Faction, A. 2018. *Faction A Sentiment Analysis Dashboard Demo*. www.youtube
.com/watch?v=R5HkXyAUUII

Ganguli, A., G. Iaquinti, M. Zhou, and R. Chacon. December 01, 2020. "Scaling
Datastores at Slack With Vitess." *Slack Engineering*. https://slack.engineering/
scaling-datastores-at-slack-with-vitess/

Gartner. 2021. "Hype Cycle for Digital Marketing 2021." www.gartner.com/en/marketing/research/hype-cycle-for-digital-marketing

IBM. 2021. "X-Force Threat Intelligence Index 2021." *IBM Security*, 50.

Kampakis, S. 2016. *What Is Wrong With Election Forecasting?* Retrieved from The Data Scientist. https://thedatascientist.com/election-forecasting/

Kampakis, S. October 22, 2018a. "What Are the Differences between Data-Driven, Data-Informed and Data-Centric?" *The Data Scientist* (blog). https://thedatascientist.com/data-driven-data-informed-data-centric/

Kampakis, S. 2018b. "The Different Tribes of Data Scientists." *The Data Scientist* (blog). November 5, 2018. https://thedatascientist.com/tribes-data-scientists/

Kampakis, S. January 07, 2019. "The Importance of Building a Data-Centric Culture." *The Data Scientist* (blog). https://thedatascientist.com/the-importance-of-building-a-data-centric-culture/

Kampakis, S. February 25, 2020a. "Why Predictive Maintenance Is the Next Big Thing in Manufacturing." *The Data Scientist* (blog). https://thedatascientist.com/why-predictive-maintenance-is-the-next-big-thing-in-manufacturing/

Kampakis, S. March 19, 2020b. "How AI and Data Science Can Help Fight COVID-19." *The Data Scientist* (blog). March 19, 2020. https://thedatascientist.com/ai-data-science-help-fight-covid-19/

Kumar, R., V. Misra, J. Walraven, L. Sharan, B. Azarnoush, B. Chen, and N. Govind. March 27, 2018. "Data Science and the Art of Producing Entertainment at Netflix." *Netflix Technology Blog*. https://netflixtechblog.com/studio-production-data-science-646ee2cc21a1

Leonhardt, D. July 28, 2000. "John Tukey, 85, Statistician; Coined the Word 'Software.'" *The New York Times* sec. U.S. www.nytimes.com/2000/07/28/us/john-tukey-85-statistician-coined-the-word-software.html

Lighthill, J. 1973. "Artificial Intelligence: A General Survey." Artificial Intelligence: A Paper Symposium. Science Research Council. https://aitopics.org/doc/classics:D8235CF9/

Mangel, M., and F.J. Samaniego. 1984. "Abraham Wald's Work on Aircraft Survivability." *Journal of the American Statistical Association* 79, no. 386, pp. 259–267. https://doi.org/10.1080/01621459.1984.10478038

McCorduck, P. 2004. *Machines Who Think*. 2nd ed. A K Peters/CRC Press. https://doi.org/10.1201/9780429258985

McCulloch, W.S., and W. Pitts. 1943. "A Logical Calculus of the Ideas Immanent in Nervous Activity." *The Bulletin of Mathematical Biophysics* 5, no. 4, pp. 115–133.

Microsoft. n.d. "What Is the Team Data Science Process?—Azure Architecture Center." https://docs.microsoft.com/en-us/azure/architecture/data-science-process/overview (accessed January 27, 2022).

Nakamoto, S. 2008. *Bitcoin: A Peer-to-Peer Electronic Cash System* 9.

National Research Council (U.S.), ed. 1999. *Funding a Revolution: Government Support for Computing Research*. Washington, D.C: National Academy Press.

Parizo, C. n.d. "What Are the 4 Different Types of Blockchain Technology?" *SearchCIO*. www.techtarget.com/searchcio/feature/What-are-the-4-different-types-of-blockchain-technology (accessed January 27, 2022).

Piatetsky-Shapiro, G. 1994. "Knowledge Discovery in Databases: Progress Report." *The Knowledge Engineering Review* 9, no. 1, pp. 57–60. https://doi .org/10.1017/S0269888900006573

"Proof-of-Stake (PoS)." n.d. *Ethereum.Org*. https://ethereum.org (accessed January 27, 2022).

Rodriguez, G. May 09, 2018. "Introduction to Recommender Systems." *Tryolabs*. https://tryolabs.com/blog/introduction-to-recommender-systems

Rogati, M. 2017. "The AI Hierarchy of Needs | HackerNoon." *Hackernoon*. https://hackernoon.com/the-ai-hierarchy-of-needs-18f111fcc007

Russell, S., and P. Norvig. 2008. http://aima.cs.berkeley.edu/

Russell, S.J., P. Norvig, and E. Davis. 2010. *Artificial Intelligence: A Modern Approach*, 3rd ed. Prentice Hall Series in Artificial Intelligence. Upper Saddle River: Prentice Hall.

Samuel, A.L. 1959. "Some Studies in Machine Learning Using the Game of Checkers." *Ibm Journal of Research and Development*, pp. 71–105.

"Semi-Supervised Machine Learning." n.d. *DataRobot AI Cloud* (blog). www .datarobot.com/wiki/semi-supervised-machine-learning/ (accessed January 27, 2022).

Solaguren-Beascoa, A. April 04, 2020. "Active Learning in Machine Learning." *Medium*. https://towardsdatascience.com/active-learning-in-machine-learning-525e61be16e5

"The Beginner's Guide to Kaggle." July 13, 2017. *EliteDataScience*. https:// elitedatascience.com/beginner-kaggle

"TradeLens | Digitizing Global Supply Chains." n.d. www.tradelens.com/ (accessed January 27, 2022).

Tukey, J.W. 1962. "The Future of Data Analysis." *The Annals of Mathematical Statistics* 33, no. 1, pp. 1–67. https://doi.org/10.1214/aoms/1177704711

"Understanding Descriptive and Inferential Statistics | Laerd Statistics." n.d. https://statistics.laerd.com/statistical-guides/descriptive-inferential-statistics .php (accessed January 27, 2022).

Whitby, B. 1996. *Reflections on Artificial Intelligence: The Legal, Moral and Ethical Dimensions*. Exeter: Intellect Books.

Willcox, W.F. 1938. "The Founder of Statistics." *Revue de l'Institut International de Statistique / Review of the International Statistical Institute* 5, no. 4, p. 321. https://doi.org/10.2307/1400906

Yu, V.L., L.M. Fagan, S.M. Wraith, W.J. Clancey, A.C. Scott, J. Hannigan, R.L. Blum, B.G. Buchanan, and S.N. Cohen. 1979. "Antimicrobial Selection by a Computer: A Blinded Evaluation by Infectious Diseases Experts." *JAMA* 242, no. 12, pp. 1279–1282. https://doi.org/10.1001/jama.1979.03300120033020

Zhou, Z.H. 2018. "A Brief Introduction to Weakly Supervised Learning." *National Science Review* 5, no. 1, pp. 44–53. https://doi.org/10.1093/nsr/nwx106

About the Authors

Dr. Stylianos (Stelios) Kampakis is a data scientist and blockchain expert with more than 10 years of experience. He has worked with decision makers from companies of all sizes: from start-ups to big organizations. He is the CEO of the Tesseract Academy.

Dr. Theodosis (Theo) Mourouzis is a cryptologist and information security professional with strong interests in both academia and industry. He holds a PhD in Information Security with Specialization in Cryptography from University College London. Theo is Managing Partner of Electi Consulting.

Gerard Cardoso is a data scientist and AI strategist whose mission is to demystify data science for the masses and unlock the value of data in every business. Gerard has spent his career advising businesses, from start-ups to large corporations on how to think about data strategy.

Dr. Marialena Zinopoulou is a lecturer for the MSc Strategic Marketing and MSc Management Program at Imperial College Business School, London, and a Guest Lecturer for University College London (UCL). She is the CEO of The Digital Marketing Association (DMA), a not-for-profit membership and education organization.

Index

OTHER TITLES IN THE BIG DATA, BUSINESS ANALYTICS, AND SMART TECHNOLOGY COLLECTION

Mark Ferguson, University of South Carolina, Editor

- *Getting Data Science Done* by John Hawkins
- *Four Laws for the Artificially Intelligent* by Ian Domowitz
- *The Data Mirage* by Ruben Ugarte
- *Introduction to Business Analytics, Second Edition* by Majid Nabavi
- *Emerging Technologies* by Errol S. van Engelen
- *Data-Driven Business Models for the Digital Economy* by Rado Kotorov
- *Highly Effective Marketing Analytics* by Mu Hu
- *Business Analytics, Volume II* by Amar Sahay
- *Introduction to Business Analytics* by Majid Nabavi and David L. Olson
- *New World Technologies* by Errol S. van Engelen
- *Business Analytics, Volume I* by Amar Sahay
- *Location Analytics for Business* by David Z. Beitz
- *Data Mining Models, Second Edition* by David L. Olson
- *World Wide Data* by Alfonso Asensio

Concise and Applied Business Books

The Collection listed above is one of 30 business subject collections that Business Expert Press has grown to make BEP a premiere publisher of print and digital books. Our concise and applied books are for…

- Professionals and Practitioners
- Faculty who adopt our books for courses
- Librarians who know that BEP's Digital Libraries are a unique way to offer students ebooks to download, not restricted with any digital rights management
- Executive Training Course Leaders
- Business Seminar Organizers

Business Expert Press books are for anyone who needs to dig deeper on business ideas, goals, and solutions to everyday problems. Whether one print book, one ebook, or buying a digital library of 110 ebooks, we remain the affordable and smart way to be business smart. For more information, please visit www.businessexpertpress.com, or contact sales@businessexpertpress.com.

www.ingramcontent.com/pod-product-compliance
Lightning Source LLC
Chambersburg PA
CBHW061311220326
41599CB00026B/4838

* 9 7 8 1 6 3 7 4 2 3 1 3 4 *